GRACE
to become

GRACE
to become

EMILY BELLE FREEMAN

Artwork by EVA KOLEVA TIMOTHY

DESERET
BOOK

Interior artwork © Eva Koleva Timothy
page x: *Grace*
page 6: *Positive Pedaling*
page 18: *Epiphany*
page 26: *Fallen Star*
page 36: *Millenial Daydream*
page 46: *Star Stretching*
page 58: *Embark*
page 70: *Dream Catching*
page 82: *Consecration*
page 92: *Loves Light*
page 102: *The Path*
page 116: *Freedom Song*

Background: Silver Spiral Arts / Shutterstock.com
Endsheets: RODINA OLENA / Shutterstock.com

DESERET BOOK is a registered trademark of Deseret Book Company.

Visit us at deseretbook.com

Library of Congress Cataloging-in-Publication Data
(CIP on file)
ISBN: 978-1-63993-005-0

Printed in China
RR Donnelley, Dongguan, China

10 9 8 7 6 5 4 3 2 1

For my Youngest One, Grace

Simply because you asked,
but mostly because your story taught me
that even when fear surrounds
and especially when the journey appears hardest,
grace shall be.

CONTENTS

CONTENTS

The Lord will meet us
where we are, as we are,
but He does not intend to leave us there;
He came to lift us up to
where He is, as He is.

THIS IS THE JOURNEY OF GRACE.

chapter one

THE JOURNEY OF GRACE

I open her text just moments after the chime sounds.

Are you home?

Life has been lonely. It has been so long since a friend stopped by. I don't even take a second to think about the disheveled state of my life and my home and my heart; I just quickly respond back.

Yes.

I am standing outside the garage when she pulls up. All is in a state of disarray. Why is it when you begin the process of cleaning out that everything becomes messier? My first instinct is to lower the great brown door to hide the overflowing boxes and the scattered bikes and the snow boots that need their match, but she is out of her car and confidently walking across the lawn before I get the chance. She raises her hand in a spontaneous wave, her smile spilling over like it always does. As her eyes grasp hold of mine, I realize she doesn't even notice the mess because of how focused she is on me. That is her way. It is one of the things I love most about her.

In her hand she holds a brown cardboard square tied with a piece of jute and gold tulle. "I had to get this for you." Her eyes sparkle with anticipation now. "As soon as I saw it, I just knew you had to have it." It isn't my birthday. I haven't done anything in our relationship recently to merit a gift, so I can't help but wonder why I deserve this generosity. But with those few words, she is done with her explanation. I tug gently on the jute, pulling the soft tulle ribbon off the edges of the cardboard, and lift the top piece. When I see the beautiful painting preserved within the cardboard, I gasp. There are no words, but there are tears, and my eyes return to hers for understanding. "I knew you would love it," she whispers. "I just knew."

Before long she returns to her car, and I hold the gift carefully in both hands as I walk through the front door.

Grace.

The name of the painting is handwritten on the white edge of the thick paper imported from France, chosen by the artist for its texture and its beauty. The quality of the paper brings the colors of the painting to life. I feel the soft thickness and get lost in the image. The wheat field, the red ladder, the girl in the yellow dress, the reaching, the glitter falling down from heaven.

I can't help but wonder which part of the painting had pierced my soul and brought about the instantaneous tears. Silence surrounds. I stand in the front hall, one long stream of light slanting through the upper window and spilling onto the artwork. The Spirit whispers soft. *It's not the yellow dress, or the reaching. It isn't how far she had to carry the old wooden ladder, or how many rungs she climbed. It's the fact that the grace spilling out of heaven would have reached her regardless.*

Unmerited.
Undeserved.
Unscheduled.

And yet, she couldn't wait.

She recognized the gift, and on that stormy afternoon, reaching out to fully embrace it became paramount.

Discourse on Abbatôn

He took the clay from the hand of the angel,
and made Adam according to Our image and likeness,
and He left him lying for forty days and forty nights
without putting breath into him.

And He heaved sighs over him daily, saying,
"If I put breath into this [man],
he must suffer many pains."

And I said unto My Father,
"Put breath into him;
I will be an advocate for him."

And My Father said unto Me,
"If I put breath into him, My beloved Son,
Thou wilt be obliged to go down into the world,
and to suffer many pains for him
before Thou shalt have redeemed him,
and made him to come back to his primal state."

And I said unto My Father,
"Put breath into him;
I will be his advocate,
and I will go down into the world,
and will fulfil Thy command."

—TIMOTHY, ARCHBISHOP OF ALEXANDRIA[1]

chapter two

LIFTED UP

"A powerful expression of that love
is what the scriptures often call the grace of God
—the divine assistance and endowment of strength
by which we grow from the flawed and limited beings
we are now into exalted beings of truth and light."

—DIETER F. UCHTDORF[2]

She struggled with infertility for years. She waited, and then waited some more, until finally it wasn't worth getting her hopes up anymore. That is when the baby came. A little boy. Oh, how she loved that little boy.

It wasn't many years later that he got sick. It started with a headache. She sat still and held him from morning until noon. And then, there in his mother's arms, he died. Surely she cried, the woman who laid him down carefully on a bed and then called out to her husband. It will be well, she said. Send for someone to drive me without slowing to Mount Carmel, until we reach the man of God.

The prophet saw her coming. He yelled for his servant to run and meet her. He counseled the servant to ask her three questions: "Is it well with thee? is it well with thy husband? is it well with the child? And she answered, It is well" (2 Kings 4:26). *Shalom*. It is well.

What?!

Every time I read the story, I stop at those words. How can it be well? My mother heart cries out with pain. It's not hard for me to imagine her running to the prophet and falling at his feet. I can hear her telling him the story with tears. The story ends when the prophet walks into her home and heals the boy and whispers, "Take up thy son" (2 Kings 4:36). But I have to be honest; my most favorite part is right there in the middle. When things are not resolved. The part when the mother whispers three words in the midst of her great trial.

No matter the outcome, because of her faith in His grace, all would be well.

⊕ ⊕ ⊕

You could have filled a vial with my tears that night. Perhaps someone in Heaven did. Life wasn't going the way I thought it would. It was broken; I was broken. Exhausted. Maybe the sun still came up every morning, but I had stopped noticing. *All was not well.* For the first time in a year that had completely fallen apart, I poured out my heart to God. I told Him what hurt, what I couldn't carry alone anymore. My soul just needed rest. Then grace came, *saving grace.* In the midst of that dark moment, sweet peace filled the room. The Spirit of the Lord. On that sacred night, the burden lifted for a time, and a portion of healing washed over my heavy heart.

Perhaps you have heard me talk of this story before, the little boy I held through the hard things. Maybe you know what it is to raise a child with a diagnosis that will last throughout mortality. In the beginning, the dread of facing that challenge again day after day had the potential to destroy me. I didn't want to get out of bed in the morning, I cried several times each day, and every night I would fall into bed with a prayer of exhaustion, pleading for His grace. Healing. Deliverance. Rescue. Every night, without fail, He would send the grace of His Son to heal me and strengthen me. To give me rest. Grace to overcome the pain. But that saving grace in and of itself was not all that was needed for my journey. It was a balm that quieted me, but I needed something more.

In those first days and months after the diagnosis my heart needed healing, but as the days went on, I realized what I would need most was to be transformed into the mother that Josh needed me to be. A mother who would sacrifice sleep in order to ensure health, who would work outside the home in order to pay medical bills, who would learn basic nursing skills in order to preserve life.

I didn't want to do any of those things; my own capacity did not qualify me for it.

But my mortality required it.

Knowing my story, God sent One willing to count the tears in the midnight hours, but also One willing to enable me and transform me to become equal to the task. To increase my capacity. To lift me. To transform me through grace into the mother whose job was to poke and prick and restrict and control while also being the mother who could comfort and encourage and bring joy.

On my own, becoming that mother was impossible.
I wasn't strong enough.
But with Him, through His transforming grace, I could.

It is what enabled me to whisper those three words of hope in the midst of my own great trial.

It is well.

No matter the outcome, because of my faith in His grace.

✠ ✠ ✠

We don't remember it now, but there was a moment when each of us left the presence of God. A piece of fruit, a garden farewell, and we were on our way. We came to mortality to till the ground that was cursed, knowing sorrow would fill all the days of our life. Thorns and thistles. Sweat and dust. We came to learn Jesus. To learn the unforced rhythms of grace. We knew there would be moments of joy, but there would also be pain. I believe we knew there would be pain.

Cancer.

Death.

Accidents.

Abuse.

The Father also knew about the pain. He saw how it would touch every single one of us.

Most often God doesn't take the broken out of mortality. He allows mortality to do its work in us, to grow us, to stretch us. That is why we are here, for the growing. Unwilling to leave us in this place alone, our God sent His Son down to a starlit stable filled with that sweat and dust. He came to meet us where we are, as we are. It was condescension—*God entering our story*. But Jesus didn't intend to leave us here. He knew we would need the saving grace that would be made available through His atoning sacrifice to get through mortality. But that was only the beginning of His great work.

His highest hope is to return us back to the presence of God.
For each of us to meet Him where He is, as He is.
This will require more than just saving. It will require exalting.

An ascension—*God finishing our story.*

Lifting.
Transforming.
Elevating a soul.

This is His work and His glory.

The wind rustled soft through the leaves of the giant tree. We settled into the shade grateful for a pause in the day. She with her black hair hanging long over her shoulders, me with a straw hat and bare feet. It was a slow afternoon. The kind where you can lean into deep conversation; the type of talking that heals a soul. She asked about Jesus, and belief, and grace. Why live a covenant life when most of the world tells you belief in Christ is sufficient?

It is a good question. One that many people are asking now. The answer to that question is one I have been seeking for years. The learning has come in seasons, precept by precept. Sometimes knowledge distills upon a soul like drops of dew. It takes time in His word, personal encounters with Christ, walking His covenant path. The greatest learning often comes through the tutoring of the Spirit as it comes and goes, whispering of heavenly things (see John 3:8–13).

"Life has led me to experience two types of grace," I told her.

"One is the grace that heals wounds. This is the grace that glitters down from heaven to meet you where you are, as you are. It is the balm of broken things, the righting of what's gone wrong, the mending of a heart. I have felt it in the midnight hours, in the struggle, in the sorrow of heavy things. This grace flows from the merits of the Atonement of Christ to help us *overcome*."

"I have also experienced a grace that elevates souls," I explained to her. "This is a grace that lifts, increases capacity, transforms us, and enables increase and progression. This grace flows from the merits of the Atonement of Christ to help us *become*."

"You and I need both," I told her. "One is felt in the moments we allow Him to enter our story. The other is felt in the moments we allow Him to finish our story. In my life, I view one as salvific and the other as exalting. Saving grace is received through belief in Christ and His atoning sacrifice. Exalting grace is also received through belief in Christ and His atoning sacrifice, but is administered by the Holy Ghost as we participate in sacred ordinances and covenants" (see D. Todd Christofferson, "Why the Covenant Path," *Liahona*, May 2021).

> Saving grace is the enabling strength to overcome.
> Exalting grace is the enabling strength to become.[3]

There are days when I am in need of saving. Healing. Fallen moments when I want nothing more than to receive His gift of grace for the healing of bitter wounds. But there are other days when I long to be transformed into a better mother, a better friend, a better wife. On those days, I yearn for an increase of capacity—although I still seek healing, deliverance, and rescue, what I need most is transformation, progression, and becoming. There is something significant in believing Jesus Christ can lift me to better living, a condition I could never arrive at on my own, and allowing His enabling strength to make it possible.

As we spoke, I watched the tears fill her eyes. "Why have I never understood this before?" she whispered. "The importance of the ordinances and covenants. They are more than what I thought. They are what enables the becoming. The exalting. Where can I learn more about this process of lifting?" she wondered.

Perhaps you wonder the same thing.

It is a beautiful truth sprinkled throughout all of scripture. You will discover it in every book of the standard works. Jesus came down to lift us up. "And my Father sent me that I might be lifted up upon the cross; and after that I had been lifted up upon the cross, that I might draw all men unto me, that as I have been lifted up by men even so should men be lifted up by the Father. . . . And for this cause have I been lifted up; therefore, according to the power of the Father I will draw all men unto me, that they may be judged according to their works. . . . [And] nothing entereth into his rest save it be those who have washed their garments in my blood, because of their faith, and the repentance of all their sins, and their faithfulness unto the end" (3 Nephi 27:14–15, 19).

No matter where you read the story of Christ, you will discover a coming down and a lifting up. Christ did not come simply to meet us where we are, as we are; He came to lift us up to where He is, as He is. He offers saving grace to heal us, but as we walk the covenant path, He also means to transform us and lift us through His gift of exalting grace.

"And I, if I be lifted up from the earth, will draw all men unto me" (John 12:32).

Upward and forward.
Increase and progression.

The fulness of this transformation will require us to grasp hold of the promise given to Abraham, to enter into the covenant path that exalts. The Father knew we would need greater guidance, greater protection, and greater inspiration for the full transformation to take place. He knew how those privileges would be magnified through priesthood ordinances and covenants. It is why He designed the path; He knew walking it would lead to the lifting and progression and increase.

As our conversation drew to a close, she asked me one more question, my friend with the dark hair and the tears glistening in her brown eyes. "Teach me what you believe about the temple because of your understanding of this grace."

Her question made me stop and consider something I hadn't before. "It's all about relationship," I realized as I spoke the words out loud. "I enter into those ordinances and covenants not out of obligation or expectation, but because of deep longing for what I hope to receive and become through Him. In the end, my goal is not to just become the best mother or friend or sister or spouse I can be in this life, but to actually become like Him. Like He is. I long for His grace to help me through mortality, to transform me into the best version of myself I can be while I am here. When all

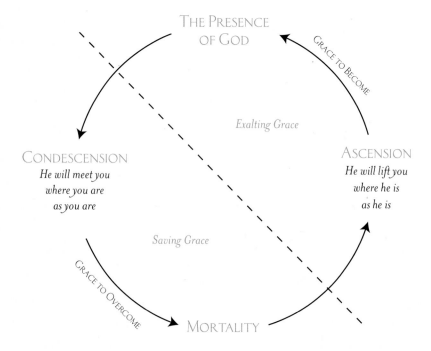

is said and done, my highest goal is to become like Him so I can return back to the Father's presence. I need more than just the grace that will strengthen me through mortality. I want to go home."

As we move along the covenant path from salvation to exaltation, Christ enables our progress through grace. His saving grace rescues us, heals us, delivers us, and helps us overcome death, sin, and the weakness of mortality. His exalting grace enables progression and increase, transformation, the ability to become as He is and eventually receive the Father's fulness.

Saving grace meets us where we are, as we are—it is grace to overcome. But Christ doesn't intend to leave us there. He plans to lift us up, to return us back to the presence of God—to where He is, as He is. For that, He offers exalting grace—*grace to become*.

Just like saving grace, this grace that elevates souls is also a gift.

If you reach out to fully embrace it, if that becomes paramount, your life will never be the same.

Stretch wide your arms, dear friend.
Look up.
His gift is showering down upon you.

Grace to become.

chapter three

WHERE THE STORY BEGINS

"We shall reach His kingdom,
where we will be lifted up to eternal life."
—RUSSELL M. NELSON[4]

Twilight was filtering in through the back windows when my phone rang. I was cutting peppers—the yellow, orange, and red gathering together in a pile on the wooden block. "Hello there!" It was a good friend, and I love a companion to talk to while I am making dinner.

"I have a question," she began. Even better. It's my friend Nish, who is a nondenominational Christian, and her questions always lead to a good conversation. On this particular afternoon, she wanted to know the difference between salvation and exaltation. "If the celestial kingdom, ordinances, the covenant path and striving for exaltation are so important," she wondered, her question sincere and honest, "why is that never mentioned in the Bible the way you talk about it?"

I don't turn away from the question, even though I'm not sure how to answer it—unknowing can open a vault for capturing God's wisdom if you allow it to be so. My friend is patient with me. She is comfortable with the unknowing. I have stumped her with my own questions a few times as well. We process the possibilities for a minute as I shred the chicken and heat up the tortillas, and then, as the family gathers in for dinner, I tell her I will do some looking and we will talk again. These questions back and forth have become the ongoing conversation of our life. They grow me. I am better for it.

The next morning, I turn to the story of God's people found in the book of Genesis. I want to discover the reason for choosing to live a covenant life, the reason I belong to a faith that teaches about exaltation. There, near the beginning, I come across a Hebrew word I have written in the margin in my messy script: *Abram*—exalted father.[5] I notice the word *exalted*, and because of the conversation with my friend, I am instantly drawn in.

I read a story that weaves together themes of weakness and faith, staggering and hope, unbelief and promise, and I wonder how Abraham held fast to a promise that was sure and a God who was able when the conditions of his life suggested otherwise.

Then Jehovah appeared to Abraham, saying, "I am thy shield, and thy exceeding great reward" (Genesis 15:1). It was a promise of protection, but also increase—*I am your saving and your exaltation.* I pause here for understanding. It is the first time I have ever noticed a scripture that contains the promise of a grace that saves and a grace that exalts. Two promises crucial to Abraham's mortal journey. But instead of immediately grasping hold of the promise, Abraham focused on his lack. There was no future in Abraham's home, no possibility for increase. Sarah was barren.

It seemed Jehovah had offered an impossible promise. In fact, the conditions of mortality ensured that Abraham could not obtain it.

But Jehovah was not hindered by Abraham's mortal inadequacy. He spoke of stars flung across the heavens, of exceeding great reward, "and [Abraham] believed in the Lord" (Genesis 15:6). But enduring faith did not come immediately. "Whereby shall I know . . . ?" Abraham questioned the Lord (Genesis 15:8).

Sometimes the only way to move forward is through grace.

A few verses down from there, Abraham's story teaches us what it looks like to live in covenant relationship. I am fascinated with the learning. The Lord instructed Abraham to obtain a heifer, a she-goat, a ram, a turtledove, and a young pigeon. It was the preparing of a covenant. In those days, it was custom to cut each sacrifice in half and place them all in a line, each half across from the other. Then the two covenanting parties would pass between them, and when both had walked through the carcasses, the promise would be sure. Instead of signing a document, this was covenant ritual. In Hebrew, the phrase "make a covenant" is *karath berith*—more precisely meaning "to cut a covenant." The walking between the pieces signified the promise, "If I do not keep my covenant, may I become as this animal."[6]

So, Abraham prepared the covenant and then waited on the Lord. All day long he waited. As morning turned to afternoon and then on to evening, Abraham drove the hovering fowls away from what was meant to be the sign of his promise.

Have you ever waited on the Lord? Have you ever wondered if His promise is too good to be true? Have you watched the sun go down on your promise and felt the weight of darkness settle in?

Exhausted, Abraham fell asleep.

When it was dark, "behold a smoking furnace, and a burning lamp . . . passed between those pieces" (Genesis 15:17). This is my favorite part of the story—in the middle of that dark place, only the Lord walked through. "Then it was that the covenant was made; not, as usually, by both parties passing between the divided sacrifice, but by Jehovah alone doing so, since the covenant was that of *grace,* in which one party alone—God— undertook all the obligations, while the other received all the benefit."[7] In that moment, the Lord placed the penalty of violating the covenant on Himself.

The covenant was that of grace.

The Lord promised Abraham that He would uphold both sides of the covenant, even if it meant the shedding of His own blood. *From the beginning He was willing to offer His life for Abraham's.* It is one of the first examples of grace recorded in the story of God's people, and there is an important lesson here. Abraham's posterity was ensured salvation through the Atonement of Jesus Christ, but there was more. His posterity was promised a path that would exalt them if they chose to enter into the covenant relationship. It was the promise of priesthood ordinances that would lead to exaltation and eternal increase. This was different than just receiving salvation— everyone in Abraham's posterity who received salvation through belief in Christ now became eligible to also receive the blessing of the Abrahamic covenant if they chose—they were entitled to this eternal increase—but they would be required to live a life worthy of obtaining it. Every blessing, through their faithfulness. A life of covenant becoming.

Because we are the children of Abraham, Jehovah offers each of us that same promise filled with impossibility. Your personal conditions of mortality, your inadequacies and weakness might make you question whether you will ever realize that promise.

Jehovah is not now, nor ever has been, hindered by mortal inadequacy.

His answer is exalting grace.

In your darkest places, look for the burning lamp. In the barren places, watch for His increase.

"I am thy shield, and thy exceeding great reward" (Genesis 15:1). His is the promise of protection *and* increase—*I am your saving and your exaltation.*

Here was the answer my friend was seeking.
An invitation to pursue exaltation found in the Bible.
An invitation for every one of us.

A thought settles into my heart.

Every so often in a life, a sudden insight into an essential truth will come from an ordinary experience. An epiphany. Our feet may be firmly planted in the dirt we have lighted upon, darkness may surround, but for a time we are given a glimpse of who we are and the potential of who we can become through grace. In those fleeting moments, the earth fills with a burning light and our fingertips trace the promise written in the stars flung wide. Then, trailing clouds of glory and encircled by His grace, we step onto our own path of becoming and begin to write our own story filled with grace, and exalting, and Him . . .

Therefore ye are justified of faith and works,
through grace,
to the end the promise might be sure . . .
to them also who are of the faith of Abraham;
who is the father of us all . . .
who against hope believed in hope . . .
and being not weak in faith . . .
he staggered not at the promise of God
through unbelief;
but was strong in faith, giving glory to God . . .
being fully persuaded that,
what [God] had promised,
he was able also
to perform.

JOSEPH SMITH TRANSLATION,
Romans 4:16–21

chapter four

THE LORD IS IN THIS PLACE

*"With the gift of God's grace,
the path of discipleship does not lead backward;
it leads upward."*

—DIETER F. UCHTDORF[8]

We always walk the same path, my dear friend and I. Almost every day we leave the neighborhood and stroll onto the path that winds through the wilderness place. Yes, the path is always the same, but the conversation never is. Today she tells me about the boy leaving for his mission who spoke in her ward last Sunday. The one who had been asked to speak on his relationship with Christ. He said writing the talk was hard for him because he had so many personal stories to choose from.

"Jesus is my oldest friend," he explained.

My heart almost beat right out of my chest when she told me. I knew exactly what that boy was talking about, but I'd never described it quite like that. Now the phrase won't leave my thoughts.

I remember Him showing up that day after my grandpa died and I sat on the curb of the playground at recess and wondered why all of the other kids were so happy.

I was seven.

He was there.

And again, when I was twelve and the girls who had always been my friends told me I wasn't cut out for the popular crowd and I walked home from the bus stop alone; He was there then too.

At seventeen, when I left everything behind for the amazing experience He called me into; at nineteen when I was the loneliest I have ever been; at twenty-six when the sky came crashing down.

Still there.

When the babies came after months and months of walking through the valley of the shadow of death, He was with us to celebrate. For me, new life always witnessed of His miracles. He smiled on us on those sacred days.

When I was diagnosed with my second melanoma and I was so sick for days, and weeks, and months, and I wondered if I would ever be whole again. When I lost my dear friend to cancer. When doubt and discouragement and failure overwhelmed.

In every single one of those moments, both the sweet celebrations and the deep sorrows, He was there. Constant. Steady. Sure. The One who kept me from falling. An ever-present help in times of trouble. The giver of grace. Jesus. For me, to live, is Christ. I don't know where I would be without Him.

That boy put into words what my heart has always known but lacked a description for. His simple words reminded me that I do not travel alone through this wilderness place. None of us do. He reminded me how important it is to stop and remember Him, the One who has been there through it all.

Jesus.

Our oldest friend.

⊕ ⊕ ⊕

It must have been a sacred moment when Isaac called Jacob, "and blessed him, and charged him" (Genesis 28:1), because Jacob didn't once question his father's advice to travel several hundred miles to find a wife. He just went.

Perhaps dusk settled in slow on that first day. I imagine a long and weary journey from Jacob's home at Beersheba to where he had arrived. Sacred words suggest an accidental arrival: "He lighted upon a certain place" (Genesis 28:11). It was a valley filled with dirt and strewn with rocks. Some might wonder if Jacob had been led there by divine design—I wonder if he knew this was the same place his grandfather Abraham had stood shoulder-to-shoulder with Lot, when Jehovah promised the land to him those many years before (see Genesis 12:7–8). Yes, this valley was a sacred place filled with promise, but it seems Jacob had stopped there simply because the sun was going down.

I have raised young adults. I have watched them pack for camping trips. When I read Jacob's story, it doesn't seem like a whole lot of planning took place. This account suggests that he came upon a random place by happenstance and decided to sleep there because it had gotten dark. *It's hard to journey through unknown wilderness places in darkness.* But there is more. The scriptures do not talk of a tent or of bedding; instead we read how Jacob took the stones of that place and used them for his pillows and lay down on the dirt to sleep.

I can imagine him there, sleeping hard after a long day's walk—only a few steps into hundreds of miles he would travel. I read of the dream filled with angel light, a ladder reaching to heaven, angels ascending and descending, and just there, next to the ladder rungs, Jehovah. *Standing beside Jacob.* Right there. In the wilderness place he had come to by chance (see Genesis 28:13, footnote b).

"I am the Lord God of Abraham, thy father, and the God of

Isaac," Jehovah whispers to the boy. *I am the God of your grandfather. The Promise Keeper.* The grandson must have found great comfort there. Then Jehovah continues, *This land that you have somehow lighted upon,* "the land whereon thou liest, to thee will I give it, and to thy seed" (Genesis 28:13).

> *Do you see the dirt where you are lying?*
> *I plan to give it to you . . . but there is more . . . I plan to bless it.*

Have you ever been in a wilderness place? Have you ever gotten yourself somewhere by chance, because of lack of planning, because someone told you to go discover something better, because the sun went down and you were exhausted, and this is simply where you gave up?

Have you ever wondered if the Lord would meet you there in that random place? Stand beside you? Point to that place and say, *You know this place where you have somehow gotten yourself to? I am planning to bless it.*

Yes. This place.

It doesn't matter how you got here. It doesn't even matter where you think you are going. In this moment, all that matters is the truth that the Lord will meet you right here in your story. Where you are. He will stand beside you and offer saving grace. *He plans to bless you.*

But that is not all.

There is more. This wilderness visit from the Lord is not a once-in-a-lifetime occurrence. The Lord tells Jacob, "Behold, I am with thee, and will keep thee in all places whither thou goest, and will bring thee again into this land; for I will not leave thee, until I have done that which I have spoken to thee of" (Genesis 28:15).

I am with thee.
I will keep thee.
I will bring you again to this place.
I will not leave thee.
I will do that which I have promised thee.

This is the whisper of Israel's covenant promise combined with the Lord's gift of grace. We read the story once as we followed Grandfather Abraham. We see it now again in the story of his grandson, Jacob. It was powerful the first time, this story that began with Grandfather Abraham, and continued with his son Isaac, and one more time in the story of the grandson Jacob. The story of a God who promises and provides and prevails. It is a story that is life-altering. But there is more. There is a greater lesson here. What the Lord told Jacob is true for you and me. Right now. Right here.

Where is your wilderness place?
Where is your dirt?

The Lord is about to bless that place.

You might feel unprepared. Perhaps you are exhausted from the efforts you have given so far. Maybe you are just a few miles into a journey hundreds of miles long, and you aren't even sure if you want to take the next step.

You should.
You will not walk the journey alone.

The morning after the dream, as the sun filtered soft into the valley, Jacob woke up and took his pillow and stood it up as a pillar. Then he named the place where he had stayed Beth-el, which means *house of God*, and he said, "Surely the Lord is in this place; and I knew it not" (Genesis 28:16).

Surely
the Lord is in this place;
and I knew it not.

Is there a chance the Lord is already in the place where you are, and you just don't know? The God of Abraham, the God of Isaac, the God of Jacob?

I love reading Jacob's story because it describes for us both saving and exalting grace. The beginning of Jacob's story is filled with *saving grace*. In that wilderness place, the Savior offered him deliverance, rescue, and healing. Grace in a valley of happenstance. Through Jacob we are reminded that the Lord will enter our stories where we are, as we are, in an effort to bless us.

But Jacob's story doesn't end with just one encounter with grace.

No, the story of the boy who used a rock for a pillow continues for twenty-one more chapters, and it is in these twenty-one chapters that we begin to see the power and the process of *exalting grace* made manifest. Jacob's story will be filled with moments of deceit and moments of glory, righting wrongs and entering covenants. We will watch a process of transformation, a process that will allow change to take place through both commandment and covenant. There will be a great wrestle with the Lord and a defining moment when Jacob becomes Israel because he has finally allowed the Lord to prevail in his life, in his story, in his journey. This last half of Jacob's story defines what his path to exaltation looked like in mortality. The becoming.

Perhaps you will take some time to study those twenty-one chapters and see what you might learn from Jacob's story about becoming through grace. Look for the moments of increase and progression. The elevating of a soul. If you read carefully, you will realize Jehovah didn't just stand beside those ladder rungs on one starlit night in Beth-el; He was with Jacob every step of the way—both in the saving and in the exalting, in moments of faith and moments of repentance, in commandment and in covenant.

The story began with grace in the midnight hours, but Jehovah walked with Jacob for all his days until, grace for grace, he became Israel. It is a truth worth holding on to, a story about building relationship. Him wanting to enter into relationship with us, us responding by turning to Him and walking in His path.

Transformation requires time, but also Him.

The One who is our oldest friend.

⊕ ⊕ ⊕

I glance again at the painting from my friend, *Grace.*

I consider the young girl in the yellow dress. I see the ladder and the angel light filtering down to the place she has somehow lighted upon. In this moment she is Abraham's granddaughter, and her own story of grace is about to take place.

I know Jehovah will stand beside her, just there next to the rungs.

There will be a wrestle, righting wrongs and entering covenants, but there will also be exalting grace.

Through her process of transformation, God will prevail. She will become Israel, one of the covenant.

This is her story.
And my story.
And yours, my friend.

Surely, the Lord is in this place.

chapter five

BELIEVE AND BECOME

*"And it came to pass that Enoch continued his speech, saying:
Behold, our father Adam taught these things,
and many have believed and become the sons of God,
and many have believed not."*

—MOSES 7:1

When the young man came running, when he fell at the Lord's feet and asked Him, "Good Master, what shall I do that I may inherit eternal life?" the Lord answered back with a question: "Why callest thou me good?" (Mark 10:17–18). His question in response to a question reminds me how the Lord loves introspection, inviting us to go deeper, making us think.

When I consider this conversation, my thoughts immediately go to eternal life, because wasn't that the original question? *What must I do to qualify for eternal life?* Does it occur to you that "Why callest thou me good?" is an interesting response to a question about eternal life? Then, as if the conversation weren't strange enough already, Jesus immediately followed His own question by explaining to the young man, "There is none good but one, that is, God" (Mark 10:18).

I can't help but wonder what Jesus was doing with that follow-up remark.

If God is good, and the boy was calling Jesus good, then did the boy know that Jesus was somehow related to God? Is that what is happening here? I think it might be. Perhaps Jesus was really asking, *Do you know who I am?* Because if the young man knows who Jesus is, and he is asking *Him* what he should do to inherit eternal life, that becomes an entirely different conversation than simply asking a teacher, or a rabbi, or a man on the street. *Lord, what would you have me to do?* (see Acts 9:6). All of a sudden, the young man's question has a lot more meaning—and so does the answer.

"Keep the commandments," Jesus told him (Matthew 19:17).

"I have since my youth," the young ruler replied.

Then Jesus stopped and looked on him. I wonder what that might have been like, felt like. I wonder at the expression on Jesus's face, because the next line in the scripture says that after beholding the boy, He "loved him" (Mark 10:21).

Jesus loved that boy.

We never see that line. Most times we get caught up in the very next question from the young man, "What lack I yet?" (Matthew 19:20). We move so fast to the part of the story we know that we forget this one simple truth. *Jesus loved him.* He didn't look down on him. He didn't count him as a failure. He didn't think to Himself, *What could I ask that would destroy this boy's chance at eternal life?*

He loved that boy.
The one standing vulnerable there in the street.
Despite his lack.

Then Jesus said, "One thing thou lackest: go thy way, sell whatsoever thou hast, and give to the poor, and thou shalt have treasure in heaven: and come, take up the cross, and follow me" (Mark 10:21).

The whisper of promise, *Thou shalt have treasure in heaven.*
But also, a great work, the taking up of the cross.
Faith and grace. An invitation to believe and become.

But instead of seeing the Lord, instead of believing His promises, the rich young ruler saw only his lack. We get to this part of the story and we are so quick to judge. We see how the boy went away sad, and we immediately assign him to failure, to a life without Christ, *and why do we do that?*

The scriptures don't ever tell us what became of that boy. Who's to say he didn't become a disciple of Christ just as Nicodemus eventually did? You will remember that Nicodemus also walked away after his first conversation with Christ (see John 3:12). And why don't we ever talk about the fact that Jesus not only told that boy to sell every single thing he owned, He told him to take up the cross? In those days taking up the cross wasn't as simple as wearing a necklace is today. The cross was the cruelest form of death the Romans could come up with. It meant humiliation and shame and pain. Excruciating pain. When Christ asked the boy to take up the cross and follow Him, He was suggesting a life that would be filled with pain, sacrifice, and adversity. Becoming the very symbol of your belief. Leaving behind everything. Giving all. Just as He did.

It wasn't easy to take up the cross.

It is not easy to take up the cross.

Perhaps you and I would have walked away too. Perhaps we would have been sad. We might have had to think about that kind of commitment for a time.

I wonder, where is your lack?
Your inadequacy?
Your failure?

What are your questions?
Where is your doubt?
What if you're not enough?

What then?

And what if the thing we are most afraid of, at the root of it all, is disappointment?

Him disappointing us.
Us disappointing Him.
Nobody wants to be a disappointment.

You could hide your face. Consider walking away. You could become consumed by what you lack. Or you could enter in.

Sometimes Jesus asks us to do hard things. Even though He loves us.

Because He loves us.

Not because He is setting us up for failure. Not to emphasize the places where we lack. Not to point out our weakness. Perhaps it is because He wants us to understand His grace. Because most times it is our lack that leads us to the receiving of His grace. The grace that elevates a soul. The very grace that will enable us to take up the cross, to become.

I see a lesson manifest in the story of the rich young ruler. Becoming requires a recognition of lack. Sometimes God asks us to become vulnerable. Entering into a process of transformation is a choice. Reaching exaltation is going to require something of us.

Believing enables becoming. Courage to walk the path comes as we hold on to the promises. Faith in the promise can overcome doubt.

Do you believe in Him? Do you believe in the power of His exalting grace to lift you and transform you and make you more? Do you believe that He will deliver you and strengthen you and bring you up and be with you along the way? Do you believe in a God who promises?

I don't know why we forget to teach the second part of this story. The part when the disciples watch the rich young ruler walk away and then turn around and ask if no one with riches will enter the kingdom of God. There is a verse about a camel and a needle, and then the most important question of the entire chapter, the question that becomes the crux of it all: "*Who then can be saved?*" (Mark 10:26).

Do you know what Jesus says?

No one by themselves.
Only *with* God.

The God who promises.
The God who provides.
The God who prevails.

"With men this is impossible; but with God all things are possible" (Matthew 19:26). It was a promise meant to overcome the doubt. Jesus knew that boy could not sell all he had and live. He would not have been capable of taking up the cross and following Christ. What had been asked of him was too hard—alone. But *with Him*, it would be possible. With Jesus. Because of His grace.

I wonder if the boy regretted walking away? With time, I like to think he might have. I hope he was drawn back into a life *with* Christ because of the whisper of promise, *the treasure in heaven*. Perhaps holding on to Abraham's promise would allow him to move past the one thing he lacked, past the doubt, and enable him to accept Christ's offer of exalting grace. To believe and then to become.

Where is your lack?

Becoming will require us to be vulnerable. It will begin with a recognition of our brokenness, our lack, our weakness. Perhaps we too will stand with our soul laid bare in the middle of the street. The process will lead to us asking that same question, *Good Master, what should I do?*

You could walk away. *You could.*

Or you could take up the cross.
Enter the covenant path. Lean into His exalting grace. Believe.

You could choose to become.

The Coming

And God held in his hand
A small globe. Look he said.
The son looked. Far off,
As through water, he saw
A scorched land of fierce
Colour. The light burned
There; crusted buildings
Cast their shadows: a bright
Serpent, a river
Uncoiled itself, radiant
With slime.

On a bare
Hill a bare tree saddened
The sky. Many People
Held out their thin arms
To it, as though waiting
For a vanished April
To return to its crossed
Boughs. The son watched
Them. Let me go there, he said.

—R. S. THOMAS[9]

chapter six

HIS WORK IN YOU

"We have a glorious destiny before us;
we are engaged in a glorious work. It is worth all our attention,
it is worth our lives and everything the Lord has put into our possession
and then ten thousand times more."

—JOSEPH F. SMITH[10]

We arrived at Sixth Crossing near Martin's Cove late in the evening. We set up camp as the wind blew, and someone started charcoal for the Dutch ovens. We gathered wood and brush and lit fires around the camp for warmth because Wyoming nights are cool. If you had looked around our camp that night you would have found burning bush in the dark of a wilderness.

The next morning the sun rose us up.
We had no idea of the journey ahead.

We pulled our carts to the start of what would be a ten-mile journey. The sun reminded us that it would be nearly a hundred degrees by the time the afternoon came. We loaded the handcarts with water, with lunch, with medical supplies.

Then we started to walk.

After several hours, I met the young man walking in bare feet.

What in the world?

"What are you doing?" I immediately asked in shock. "Where are your shoes?"

"I didn't bring any," was his reply. "I wanted to learn something here about the ones who walked this path with no shoes. I figured the best way to learn that lesson was to walk the path the way they did."

To walk the path.
Vulnerable.
On a hundred-degree day.

All because of the promise of what he would learn, because of who he would become at the end.

I saw the young man again later that evening. His feet were still bare. I watched his face in the firelight and when I saw peace there I knew he had accomplished the great thing. Within the vulnerability, he had become.

I can't help but consider my own story. I want to learn something about the One who walked the dusty paths of mortality in sandaled feet. Perhaps the best way to learn is to walk the path the way He did.

Because of who I want to become.

☩ ☩ ☩

In the very moment when the bush caught fire, the Lord told Moses to put off his shoes and to stand on holy ground in the midst of a desert place. Who takes off their shoes in the desert? It is unwise. It is risky. It renders one vulnerable. But it was there, in the place where Moses stood vulnerable, that the Lord poured out the whisper of His covenant promise: "I am the God of thy father, the God of Abraham, the God of Isaac, and the God of Jacob" (Exodus 3:6). The God who promises. The God who provides. The God who prevails.

And Moses hid his face . . . (Exodus 3:6).

But his doubt didn't stop the Lord. "I have surely seen the affliction of my people which are in Egypt," He continued, "and have heard their cry by reason of their taskmasters; for I know their sorrows; And *I am come down* to deliver them . . . *and to bring them up . . . and I will send thee . . . I will be with thee . . .* Thus shalt thou say unto the children of Israel, The Lord God of your fathers, the God of Abraham, the God of Isaac, and the God of Jacob, hath sent me unto you" (Exodus 3:7–15; emphasis added).

I am the coming down.
I am the bringing up.

The phrase whispers again of the promise given to Abraham.

I am your saving and your exaltation.

I will be with you, He promised Moses, "And it shall come to pass, that, when ye go, ye shall not go empty" (Exodus 3:21).

The whisper of grace.

Moses received the Sinai covenant at the top of an exceedingly high mountain, when God lowered the heavens and covered the mount. It was a sacred conversation that took place at the summit. I can't help but wonder about the particulars of what happened on that day when God called Moses to climb into the peaks, the journey of it, *and how long did it take to climb so high?*

"And God spake unto Moses, saying: Behold, I am the Lord God Almighty . . . And, behold, thou art my son . . . And I have a work for thee, Moses, my son" (Moses 1:3, 4, 6). Then God showed Moses the workmanship of His hands, and spoke to Him of His Only Begotten, "full of grace and truth."

I have a work for you.

"And thou shalt be made stronger," the Lord promised Moses,

"And lo, I am with thee, even unto the end of thy days; for thou shalt deliver my people from bondage, even Israel my chosen" (Moses 1:25–26). The work Moses was given was to deliver the people. Within the great commission I hear the whisper of grace that meets you where you are and grace to become. *I am with you; thou shalt be made stronger.*

The workmanship of God's hands, His people, would become the lifework of Moses. We read about the forty years in the wilderness and know that work was hard. Difficult. Transforming the children of Israel would take effort and time and would *only* be accomplished with the help of His Only Begotten, who is full of grace.

This type of becoming would require walking the path; it would require a climb.

She sat on the second row, the young girl in the yellow dress with freckles splashed across her nose. Her brown hair hung loose over her shoulders as she shifted in her seat to get a better view of the prophet. The name written on the white tag pinned to her dress read "Pearl."

"Ummm," she began, her voice gentle, hesitant. "Is it hard to be a prophet? Are you, like, really busy?"

The hint of a smile tugged at the corner of his mouth as

he began to reply, "Of course it's hard. Everything that has to do with becoming more like the Savior is difficult." President Nelson's eyes turned more serious then. "When God wanted to give the Ten Commandments . . . where did He tell Moses to go? Up on top of a mountain. . . . The Lord loves effort, because effort brings rewards that can't come without it. . . . We're always progressing."[11]

Effort leads to progression, the prophet said. *Becoming more like the Savior can be difficult.* Perhaps as you consider this idea of progression, of moving upward and forward, you recognize the difficulty, and you wonder which is the part of work and which is the part of grace.

Could it be true that you rarely have one without the other?

For if it is the Father's work, you should expect the Father's grace—to make you stronger, to increase your capacity, to enable you to fulfill the measure of your creation, to become. Effort does not qualify us for grace; instead, the prophet tells us effort leads to progression. By our own merit we cannot climb the mountain to exaltation. With faith and with the grace of Christ, by His merit and His mercy, we can (see 2 Nephi 2:8).

I wish I could have been there for the sermon that followed the request from the Apostles to the Lord: "Increase our faith" (Luke

17:5). I wanted to be there when He spoke of tiny mustard seeds and giant sycamine trees. I long to understand the relationship between grace and faith. After He was done teaching, the Lord walked with the Apostles to Jerusalem, to a certain village, to ten lepers who cried out to the Lord for mercy. "When he saw them, he said unto them, Go shew yourselves unto the priests. And it came to pass, that, *as they went,* they were cleansed" (Luke 17:14; emphasis added).

As they went.

I see the effort required there, but it was not their action alone that produced the desired result. If it were that easy, those ten men would have simply walked to the priests long before Christ entered their story. It was His divine intervention *combined* with their faith that produced the miraculous result, the transformation. Both the faith that moved the possessor to action and the touch of divine grace or favor. Faith was manifest *as they went,* but grace is what actually enabled the miraculous transformation to take place.

Faith is Peter getting out of the boat, the woman reaching for Christ's robe, the friends breaking up the roof, Zacchaeus climbing the tree. Faith is seven dips in the river Jordan, the brother of Jared carrying sixteen stones to the top of the mountain, and Moses stretching out his hand over the Red Sea. But faith, by itself, could not produce the desired outcome in any of these experiences. It was

His power that enabled the walking on water, the healing, the overcoming, the building of relationship, the cleansing, the light, the opening up of an obstructed way. His enabling strength. His grace. Faith requires action on the part of the individual. Grace is His miraculous work in us.

Perhaps elevating a soul requires a synergistic relationship. We covenant to act with faith. He promises to respond with grace.

Within the synergy, the power of Jesus Christ increases our capabilities.

Transformation is the result.

⊕ ⊕ ⊕

It is January, and I lay out a fresh piece of paper in front of me with the intention to set new goals, to contemplate the work of this new year, and I wonder what it will be. I always include the Lord in this process of soul searching. I write down the responsibilities of my life—mother, wife, grandmother, mother-in-law, friend, teacher, minister, author, creator, lifter of hearts. *What is my great work right now?* I ask the Lord. *How will I move forward and upward in each of these areas? Where do I need to be transformed? Who will I become?*

It happens every year just the same—I immediately see my lack in every situation I have listed. It is not hard to recognize failing. Weakness. I know where I am not enough. I don't mean to fail, but often failure is a natural consequence of trying. The truth about failure is that it always turns my heart to Him. I have proved Him in my lack before, in my places of want; I have handed Him my weakness and pled for His grace. It happens every single time I list my goals. I know that I can plan and prepare, but only He can bring the increase I am seeking (see 1 Corinthians 3:6). The lifting up. The progression.

Every year in January, I ask to know my great work, and then I prepare to walk the path. Over time I have learned that my effort combined with His grace offers a fertile ground for becoming.

"In the third month . . . Moses went up unto God, and the Lord called unto him out of the mountain, saying, Thus shalt thou say to . . . the children of Israel; Ye have seen . . . how I bare you on eagles' wings, and brought you unto myself. . . . And ye shall be unto me . . . an holy nation" (Exodus 19:1–6).

Sometimes upward and forward requires the wings of eagles, often bearing up requires His lifting, and holy is something we will one day be. Some people would call that miraculous; perhaps those who have experienced it would call it exalting. *A process made possible through grace—the enabling strength beyond your own to take you to a place you couldn't arrive at on your own.* The eagle wings, the bearing up, the bringing out, the being made holy are all God's promise of grace to covenant Israel.

"And the Lord called Moses up to the top of the mount; *and Moses went up*" (Exodus 19:20; emphasis added).

Where is your mountain?
What is your great work?

How is the Lord transforming you?

Take off your shoes.

chapter seven

THE UNFORCED RHYTHMS OF GRACE

"The job will not be complete in this life,
but he means to get us as far as possible before death."

—C. S. LEWIS[12]

I remember a time when religion felt heavy.

It wasn't just religion; it was life that was heavy.

I remember the day my card was declined in the grocery checkout, and how we desperately needed the food in those bags in the cupboard at home. I remember Greg not having a job. I remember feeling like God had forgotten about the job, and the empty cupboards, and the credit card that was declined.

That Sunday, I walked in to teach my Primary class and I was exhausted from life, and from worry, and from trying to make ends meet. What I didn't have was patience for other people's children, for lessons that wouldn't fill me, for hours at church that wouldn't bring answers.

Where was God?

I still remember that Sunday morning. The cold folding chair. The kids crawling all over each other. The tears welling up in my eyes because it just wasn't what I needed. It wasn't that the sanctuary didn't offer what I needed. It was that life was too heavy for me to care. It was an emptiness that couldn't be filled. A heaviness that couldn't be carried. I sat through all the hours of church that day and went home cold.

I wonder if that has ever been you?

It's hard to feel welcome in someone's house when you feel like you've been forgotten.

You probably wonder why I went back to church the next Sunday.

It is because of the yoke.

Some people view the yoke as a burden, heavy, confining, constricting, controlling. Jesus says it makes things light, that it brings rest. Which one is right?

Almost two decades ago there was another man who must have felt the same heaviness that I did, because he read the same verses that I have read a hundred times, Matthew 11:28–30, and then he rewrote those New Testament verses in his own words—*and sometimes reading the same phrase a different way from a different perspective can be life-altering.*

"Are you tired? Worn out? Burned out on religion? Come to me. Get away with me and you'll recover your life. I'll show you how to take a real rest. Walk with me and work with me—watch how I do it. *Learn the unforced rhythms of grace.* I won't lay anything heavy or ill-fitting on you. Keep company with me."[13] It is the *unforced rhythms of grace* that capture my heart when I read this passage. I want to consider each word. Unforced. Rhythms. Grace. *How to recover a life.*

I begin by thinking about the word *unforced,* because what I felt on that cold folding chair was forced, and I immediately wondered what was wrong with that place, with that situation, with those people. It didn't take long before I realized it wasn't religion that had changed; it was me. The yoke wasn't supposed to be ill-fitting or heavy. I could actually look back and remember seasons when attending church had filled me, enriched me, and lifted me. It just wasn't happening now.

No one ever said that religion was comfortable, and growing muscle requires repetition that causes pain, and strength comes from pushing ourselves outside of comfort zones, and grace is what happens when Christ enters into the empty places and into the heavy places. *Grace is what happens when Christ enters in.* Just because we don't see Him doesn't mean He isn't there. It just means we don't recognize Him in this situation. This is important. Don't be afraid to look for Him in heavy situations.

One of His best jobs is lifting.

Heavy doesn't have to mean forced. Instead, it might remind us of the need for the yoke. The sharing of the burden. Someone to help us lift the hard things. Someone to help lift us. The process of ascension requires lifting, and there is One who is willing to help. He invites us into a rhythm of enabling grace through His yoke.

The rhythm of grace.

In those moments when we feel tired of the obligation, of the requirement, of the routine, perhaps we might ask ourselves, *is there an importance to rhythm?* In doing things again, and again, and one more time? Can the rhythm of ritual worship, the repetition of it, heal us, strengthen us, lift us? Instead of being exhausting, could the rhythms actually be exhilarating? Could rhythms of unforced grace restore life?

It was shortly after that heavy season that I became very sick. I was so sick I didn't know if I would ever heal. One day Greg walked me out of the house and buckled me into the front seat of our car. He placed a pillow behind my head and then he drove me thirteen hours to the ocean. For three days I sat in the sun on the sandy beach and listened to the waves rolling in and the tide going out. There is something about that rhythm that renews the soul and restores life. And heals. And fills empty places. And lightens the burden of heavy things. For the first time in months, I knew I would recover.

The Creator must know about how rhythms heal souls, because He invites us to create rhythms in our own lives. Holy rhythms of prayer and scripture study and taking the sacrament and ordinances and covenants. These are the rhythms that rejuvenate and restore with time. Rhythms of a yoke that lifts and lightens and offers rest. They become unforced rhythms when our heart is yearning for Him.

I wonder, Do these rhythms have a place in your life?

Get away with me, He says. Rest in me. I will help you recover your life.

Keep company with me.

Learn the unforced rhythms of grace.

⊕ ⊕ ⊕

It is spring, and we are in Israel. I think of the rhythm of ritual as I dip my feet into the waters of Jordan, the waters where Naaman washed himself seven times to rid himself of leprosy. As my feet fully slip under the water, my good friend asks the question that will forever change that story for me. "Which dip was the one that healed him?"

Naaman was the captain of the host of the king, a mighty man of valor. Through him the Lord had given deliverance unto Syria. But Naaman was also a leper. So much strength, such a mighty man, able to deliver a whole country, but unable to overcome this. It was the little maid who suggested he go talk to the prophet in Samaria. "Thus and thus said the maid that is of the land of Israel" (2 Kings 5:4).

So, Naaman sent word to the prophet. The answer for Naaman's healing came through the prophet's messenger. The prophet didn't even take the time to talk with the captain, and this made the mighty man mad. It felt cold. It wasn't what he needed. It was as if the prophet didn't care. But perhaps the prophet knew that much more than healing was needed here. This was between Naaman and God. There was a process of becoming that was about to take place in this story, as well as a process of healing. Exalting and saving. A *rhythm* of grace. *Wash yourself seven times in the river Jordan.* Again, and again, and one more time. The call from the prophet was simple and clear, but Naaman hesitated. Perhaps he felt forced. Besides, the rivers of Damascus were so much cleaner. The leper wanted to choose his own way, his own healing, his own course, his own rhythm. He didn't want the yoke. So, the captain of the host went away in a rage. It was his servant that turned him back. "Then went he down, and dipped himself seven times in Jordan, according to the saying of the man of God: and his flesh came again like unto the flesh of a little child, and he was clean" (2 Kings 5:14).

Which dip was the one that healed him?

There was a rhythm in the dipping. Again, and again, and one more time. I read that story and think to myself that perhaps there is a process that leads to the presence of God. The more I study, it seems we do not become fully transformed with one encounter. Could it be the sum of every encounter that in time renders us whole? Is it the process that enables us to return to where He is, as He is? Learning Jesus. Does it come through rhythms of grace?

Perhaps every encounter with His yoke leaves the mark of grace. Through the sorrow and sweat and dust. In the blood and faith and turning again to Him. Without the yoke it would be impossible, exhausting, futile. No one can dwell in the presence of God but through the merits, mercy, and grace of Jesus (see 2 Nephi 2:8).

There is no other way to the presence of God but through exalting grace.

Grace is the divine influence to regenerate, sanctify, inspire action, impart strength, fortify endurance, resist temptation, and make us to become.[14] It is the becoming I am focused on now. The gift of His yoke for the process of exalting, for the becoming as He is. Strength will be required for the lifting up. Mine and His. It will take both of us, the process that leads to the presence of God.

It is a process that doesn't just take place in one encounter. Seven dips.

There is a rhythm and a routine.

And which one will render us like Him?

I think of what Naaman must have looked like when he rose up out of the water that seventh time, whole, and I can't help but wonder what we will look like when we finally return to His presence.

Have you ever wondered what perfection looks like?

Recently I have come to believe that our idea of perfection might not look like His. Perhaps we think perfect means in pristine condition, no marks, no mistakes, no mess. But then I remember how the process of condescension included a stable and a cross, blood and sweat, pain and sacrifice. It was messy. Will the process of ascension, the lifting up, look the same? Messy?

Will the work of becoming leave its mark on us?

⊕ ⊕ ⊕

My son had been on his mission for seven hundred and twenty days when he emailed home. "Should I throw these out?" There was a picture of his mission shoes, in prime condition when we had pulled them out of the box twenty-three months earlier. Polished. Pristine. *Isn't that what perfect looks like?* Now they were scuffed up, stitching coming undone, a hole worn through the leather by his big toe. I could see the ground through the one-inch holes scattered throughout the soles. *This is what two years looks like*, I thought to myself. *It leaves a mark.* When I saw those shoes, I could imagine the rhythms of his routine. The repetition every day. The taking of the yoke for those two years. I could imagine the stairs he had climbed, the roads he had traveled, the doors he had stood in front of, the rain he had walked through, the blood and sweat and pain and sacrifice. It wasn't hard to imagine the rhythm of growing, lifting, exalting that had taken place over those two years. The progression. The increase. I saw it manifest in those shoes. "No," I told him. "Don't throw those out. Bring them home."

In my mind, those shoes represent what perfection looks like.

Perhaps becoming is supposed to leave a mark on us.

What if finished is actually meant to include pain, and blood, and sweat, and tears? If that is true, then in the moments when life feels too much for us on our own, we must remember that some growth can be accomplished only with the strength of the yoke, His yoke, with Him and the rhythm of His grace.

Now I keep those shoes in the room where I write as a reminder that I want to look like that when my work is through. I want to have experienced all of it. I want the mark of His yoke. I want the unforced rhythm of grace to have done its work in me. I told my husband, Greg, that when I die, I want him to write four words on my tombstone: "Wasted and worn out." That's how I want to return home, with the sum of every encounter having left a mark on my soul. This learning Jesus, this drawing to Him, this growing in grace, this taking of the yoke, I want it to mark me. Every single encounter. Not only the saving grace of Him coming down to meet me where I am, as I am, but also the exalting grace, the lifting me up to meet Him where He is, as He is.

The unforced rhythms of grace.

I long for the healing, but also the becoming.

Perhaps there is a process that leads to the presence of God.

chapter eight

GRACE TO YOU

"The grace of our Lord be with you all."

—ROMANS 16:24

He must have been very wealthy, the man Paul wrote to from prison. It seems he owned a lot of land and oversaw many servants. Paul called him dearly beloved, a fellow labourer. He was someone Paul made mention of always in his prayers.

"Grace to you . . ." (Philemon 1:3).

It's how Paul begins the letter to Philemon that is found in the New Testament. It's a letter we rarely read, from a book of scripture that is only one page long, and sometimes I wonder if we don't embrace this story because the writing style and the language make it so hard to understand. However, as hard as it is to understand, Philemon happens to be my most favorite page of scripture in the New Testament. Because the language is so hard, I wonder if you would mind if I shared this story with you in my own words? I will include some of the original verses so you can mark our place in the story as we go. Perhaps you have experienced a moment when your capacity has been stretched too thin. If so, you will adore this beautiful story of grace and the powerful lesson it contains.

"Grace to you" (Philemon 1:3). It is an interesting way to begin a letter, with a prayer for grace, and I hear the whisper of something hard ahead. A defining moment that will require strength beyond Philemon's own capacity. Transformation.

Before you read on, Paul tells Philemon, *I want to strengthen your faith by asking you to remember and acknowledge every good thing that is in you because of Christ. I wish I were going to ask you to do something convenient,* Paul continues, *but I'm not. I come to you as an old man and as a prisoner, humbly, for love's sake* (see Philemon 1:4–9).

Every time I begin reading the book of Philemon, I am immediately swept up into this one-page story. It speaks to my soul. It pulls at my heartstrings. It's because I, too, have been asked to do hard things for love's sake. I have experienced moments so heavy that they have caused me to sit down and list every good thing that was mine because of Christ in order to find strength to continue on. There have been situations I wanted to turn away from because they were too big for me, because they asked too much of me, because the entering in had the potential to break me.

I feel for Philemon.

I have stood in his shoes before.

One time there was a young man who stood on the front porch of my home asking for grace after spending time in jail. I know from personal experience that what Paul is about to ask is a choice that doesn't come easy. When I read this story, I think Paul knew what he was about to ask Philemon was too great. It's why he began the letter the way he did.

Grace to you.

Grace to overcome and grace to become.

The grace that heals *and* the grace that transforms.

Both would be needed here.

"I beseech thee for my son Onesimus," he begins, and then Paul enters into the asking of the hard things (Philemon 1:10). *I met him in prison,* he explains. *You know who he is; it is a servant of yours who in times past was unprofitable* (see v. 11).

We don't know the details of the earlier relationship, we don't know what made this servant so unprofitable to Philemon, we aren't really sure why the servant left. The only detail that we have is that the servant met Paul in prison. We are left to imagine for ourselves what landed him there. Paul acknowledges the fault in the servant, the fact that he was unprofitable. Then he tells Philemon how the man has changed, saying he is "now profitable to thee and to me" (Philemon 1:11).

I sent him to you hoping you would receive him as one of my own, Paul continues. *I would have kept him with me because he was a minister to me in a time of need, but I did not know your mind. If you allow him to return to me, I want it to be willingly, not because you feel like you have to. And maybe he had to depart from you for a season; maybe there were things he needed to learn before you could receive him back home forever* (see Philemon 1:12–15).

It is when you arrive at verse 16 that the hardest ask comes. *I want you to receive him,* Paul explains, "not now as a servant, but above a servant, a brother beloved, specially to me" (Philemon 1:16). It is there within the asking that we discover the crux of the matter, because this man had wronged Philemon. He had been unprofitable. Perhaps the leaving left Philemon in a bind. The other servants had surely seen and felt the repercussion of what had been unprofitable. Now Paul was asking Philemon to take him back? And not as a servant. *As a brother.* Someone who would eat at his table, and sleep in his house, and experience all the fulness of the family.

Grace to you.

"If thou count me . . . a partner," Paul begs, "receive him as myself. If he hath wronged thee, or oweth thee ought, put that on mine account. . . . I will repay it" (Philemon 1:17–19).

There are some debts that can't be paid.
There are some wrongs that can't be righted.
There is hurt from which you don't know if you will ever heal.

Put that on my account . . . I will repay it.

Grace to you.

And then the letter concludes, "Yea, brother, let me have joy of thee in the Lord . . . having confidence in thy obedience . . . knowing that thou wilt also do more than I say. . . . Prepare me also a lodging: for I trust that through your prayers I shall be given unto you. . . . *The grace of our Lord Jesus Christ be with your spirit*" (Philemon 1:20–22, 25; emphasis added). I love how the letter ends, in the very same way it began, with a prayer for grace.

I don't even have words.

What if someone who wronged you showed up at your door with a letter in hand? A letter signed by Jesus Christ. Perhaps it might begin like this . . .

Grace to you,
For love's sake I beseech thee for this person who has wronged
you so deeply that he has spent time in prison. I know he
has been unprofitable to you, but he has changed.

I have sent him again, asking that you would receive him as one
of my own. Receive him, not as the person you once knew, but
as a brother beloved, especially to me. In fact, receive him as
you would receive me. Take care of him in that same way.

If he has wronged you, or if he owes you something for the pain
he has caused you, put that on my account; I will repay it. Let
me have joy in you in this. I have confidence in your obedience.
I know you; I know that you will actually do more than I ask.

In the meantime, prepare a place for me. I know this will be hard for
you, but I trust that through your prayers I shall be given unto you.

My grace will be with your spirit.
Jesus

Every time I read this story, I ask myself whose story of grace
this is.

Is it there in Paul, who knows what it is to be the troublemaker,
to be changed through grace, to be transformed? Paul, who can

ask Philemon to increase his capacity in this situation because he knows firsthand the power of what exalting grace can do.

Is it there in Onesimus, the man Christ met where he was, as he was, in prison with Paul, who is now in the process of allowing that transformation of grace to take place in his own life?

Is the hope of it in Philemon, who hasn't even started the transformation yet, who just received the invitation, who will have to plead for his capacity to be strengthened, for transforming grace in order to walk this road with Onesimus?

It is a powerful one-page story that leaves me asking every single time, *Whose capacity is being stretched the most?*

Whose story of grace is this?

Could it be mine?
Is it yours?

I wonder, Where is your capacity being stretched right now?

✠ ✠ ✠

When my best friend died, every project was put on the back burner. Dying brings the lives of those affected to a standstill, and for a window of time I was frozen in the process of letting someone go. Nothing else mattered.

Nothing else mattered.

But when it was over, all of the projects that had been put on the back burner resurfaced again with heated intensity. One day I turned around and it was all on top of me, boiling over.

A few days after the funeral, I finally acknowledged the deadlines and made a plan for the catching up and tried to move forward again. The assignments were all good things, but I felt the weight of them pressing down hard. Every morning I woke up and pled with the Lord, "Please, increase my capacity." That phrase became the whisper on my lips with every passing hour of those days. There were just too many things.

I was desperately in need of a priesthood blessing, but Greg was hundreds of miles away and had been for fifteen days, and I was alone in the catching up that consumed every waking hour and even the sleeping ones sometimes. As much as I needed that blessing, I resigned myself to wait.

Then, one morning, I was listening to Elder David A. Bednar on the CES broadcast for seminary teachers because it was just one more thing to check off my to-do list. There, at the very end, was the whisper of God's grace. "To anyone who is listening, wherever you are in the world . . ." And that was me, standing in my bathroom, curling my hair, preparing to teach my institute class, which was starting in fifteen minutes. "I leave you my blessing," he said, *an apostolic blessing*, and I needed a blessing so desperately. What I didn't need more of at that time was my own effort. The effort was exhausting me. I simply needed grace. I remember the tears flowing over and the realization that somehow the Lord had remembered me and my desire for a blessing and that He had found me and met me, *right there where I was.*

"In your desire to serve you will be magnified and enlarged and your capacity will be illuminated and strengthened and your capacity will be enriched. It will bless your individual life, your family, and those who you will serve now and forever."[15]

In that defining moment, I was reminded of the Lord's ability to increase my capacity.

Grace to you.

I wish I could convey to you how strongly I feel this, how deeply I believe that the Lord will meet you where you are, as you are, but that He doesn't intend to leave you there. How He plans to lift you to where He is, as He is.

This is His work and His glory (see Moses 1:39).

Both the saving and the exalting.

This transforming won't be easy, but the Father never planned for it to be. He knew it would cause reaching moments, and painful stretching, and even our tears sometimes. He also knew it would require the offering of His Only Begotten Son, a great sacrifice, and even *His* tears sometimes. It would require both saving and exalting grace.

Do you hear the whisper of something hard ahead?
Does what you have been asked to do feel too great?
Where is your capacity being stretched right now?

Grace to you.

chapter nine

FALLING SHORT

"I testify that in this and every hour
He is, with nail-scarred hands,
extending to us that same grace,
holding on to us and encouraging us,
refusing to let us go until we are safely home."

—JEFFREY R. HOLLAND[16]

It is October 2019. That young man who once stood on my front porch asking for grace now calls me mom. He moved past jail to attending college, getting married, becoming a father, and playing in the NFL. I won't forget the football season that was filled with failure and angry crowds. The mistakes you wish would remain private are touted on video and on television, and the media is relentless about everything that is broken in a boy.

Six security guards walk us out of the stadium on one occasion because his falling short has made everyone so mad.

I wonder if your falling short, your weakness, your struggles, your failures, have ever made anyone mad.

Waking up in the morning is hard. Facing a new day is hard. Even entering into normal, routine situations is hard.

He sits at the kitchen counter as I make an omelet. Home is a refuge, and we are taking a break from it all, just for a few days. His wife holds the baby on the couch. "Momma," he says after a long silence, "why has the Lord blessed me with this hard season?"

Immediately his wife exclaimed, "Why did you just use the word *blessed*?"

We laugh. And then we wonder.

Why does the Lord bless people with hard seasons?

With moments that accentuate our falling short?

If life is all about becoming, then where does falling short fit into God's plan?

✦ ✦ ✦

Jesus stood right there in the treasury and saw her poverty, her falling short, how destitute she was as she faithfully put her last two mites into the same vessel that was overflowing with everyone else's wealth. He saw that, and He still allowed it to happen. He stood back and watched the widow give all that she had, even all her living (see Mark 12:44).

Because of her want.

We learn that the widow was not the only one who came into the treasury that day. There were others who came into that place. Perhaps they came out of habit born of culture, and tradition, and expectation. *It's just what you do.* It wasn't want-based; it was routine. There were probably many who entered that day simply to check something off their list of things to do. The process did not grow them or strengthen their relationship with the Lord. They gave because they had, they gave of their abundance. There was no reason not to.

Contrast that with a woman who had probably thought things through in great detail that morning before she left her home. This was all she had. It was all her living. I wonder if she questioned, *Do I use this money for bread, or do I go hungry and give this to the Lord?* Why would she choose to go hungry? *Why?* And what were the thoughts running through her head as she walked to the temple that morning, as she approached the vessel overflowing with everyone else's abundance? Did her steps slow as she reached the giant vessel? Did her hand clutch those two mites desperately before they slipped through her fingers and into the great abundance there? Were her two mites really even necessary? In the big scheme of things, what difference would they make?

I can't help but wonder what the widow understood in that moment at the treasury. Perhaps want, or falling short, teaches one principle that is hard to come by in any other way.

His grace will make up the difference.

Maybe you have never thought about the cost of that one word. How grace makes up the difference of falling short, and being destitute, and places of poverty. Grace is what you long for deep in your soul when what you are and have and qualify for is not enough.

What is the cost of grace?

We don't have the opportunity to ask the widow about her experience. We know the extent of her poverty at the treasury, but we don't know how her story ends. Maybe she represents each of us in that regard. Perhaps you stand in the treasury with the choice of dropping in your two mites or going hungry. It could be that you are in a place of want, of falling short, and you wonder how your story is going to end.

I believe resilience and discipleship and exaltation are forged in the fire of falling short. I've met the Lord in the treasury. In my places of poverty. He showed up because of my want and offered His enabling grace.

What is the cost of grace?

Because the treasury exacts a cost, and I have felt the burden of that cost. I have clutched those two mites desperately. I have sacrificed all and then prayed desperately for His grace to make up the difference.

Who pays the cost of grace?

✠ ✠ ✠

The box arrived at my door unexpected. I hadn't ordered this package. The painting was sent as a gift. It is a giclee, limited-print copy of a young fourteen-year-old boy sitting on the floor reading his scriptures by the light of a candle. Joseph. It is breathtaking in its simplicity. I have never seen anything quite like it before.

What a beautiful gift.

"I know you love a good backstory," the giver of the gift wrote at the very bottom of the letter. It is a postscript. *Why is it that sometimes the postscripts are the very best part?* Her father-in-law had been commissioned to paint this piece for a man in 1984, she explained. The man must have tired of the painting, because somehow it ended up at a local Texas antique shop. It had become an item no one wanted anymore. Until, coincidentally, she happened to visit that very antique shop, discover the painting, and realize that it was her father's work. She wrote, "*Brother Joseph* was meant to be found by its original creator," and I smile at the double imagery happening there. She decided to purchase the painting, and I stop my reading to imagine how that conversation must have gone, because in my mind she has more ownership of that painting than the man who runs the shop. *Her father created it.* But through negotiations, she buys back the painting for $600. And I think to myself, Why in the world would someone purchase something they created for that much money?

Who pays the price of the workmanship of his own hands? *At what cost?*

It depends how great the want is.

"And Jesus sat over against the treasury, and beheld how the people cast money into the treasury: and many that were rich cast in much. And there came a certain poor widow . . ." (Mark 12:41–42).

"And he looked up . . ." (Luke 21:1).

Jesus. At the treasury. Willing to cast in more than they all, all that He had, even all His living. Because of *your* want. The purchase of your life for the cost of His.

Your poverty, your falling short.

We might believe the cost of grace is all our living, but perhaps, in reality, it is all of His. He gave all His living, His life, to redeem ours. The cost of grace is sacrifice. The Father giving His Son. The Son giving His life. Each of us turning over our life *as is* to Him. We surrender all our living, our want, our poverty, our falling short, believing that He will make up the difference, He will help us overcome, He will help us become, through grace.

Many years ago, I studied an article about grace written by Elder Bruce C. Hafen in the *Ensign*. I memorized a quote from that article that I have carried in my heart ever since. He tells us that "a sense of falling short or falling down is not only natural, but essential to the mortal experience." Then Elder Hafen teaches of grace, bestowed through the Atonement of Jesus Christ, which "can fill that which is empty, straighten our bent parts, and make strong that which is weak."[17]

I love how he reminds us that falling short is not only natural, but essential to our journey in mortality. I believe it is our falling short that causes us to yearn for a relationship with Jesus Christ. In my own experience, it is my weakness that prompts me to reach out to Him and plead for His grace. Those weak moments are what activated the full power of Jesus Christ in my life.

Sometimes we think increase and progression and exaltation come at too high of a cost. The yoke. The rhythm. We hold those mites so tightly in our fist.

Until we look around the treasury and see Him and then we know it *is* worth casting in all we have, *all our living*, because of our want:

To return to where He is.

As He is.

Patient Trust

Above all, trust in the slow work of God
We are quite naturally impatient in everything
to reach the end without delay.
We should like to skip the intermediate stages.
We are impatient of being on the way to something unknown,
something new.

And yet it is the law of all progress
that it is made by passing through some stages of instability—
And that it may take a very long time.

And so I think it is with you;
Your ideas mature gradually—let them grow,
let them shape themselves, without undue haste.
Don't try to force them on,
as though you could be today what time
(that is to say grace and circumstances
acting on your own good will)
will make of you tomorrow.

*Only God could say what this new spirit
gradually forming within you will be.
Give Our Lord the benefit of believing
that his hand is leading you,
and accept the anxiety of feeling yourself
in suspense and incomplete.*

—Pierre Teilhard de Chardin, S. J.
(1881-1955)[18]

chapter ten

THE YIELDING OF A HEART

"Yea, come unto Christ, and be perfected in him,
And deny yourselves of all ungodliness . . .
And love God with all your might, mind and strength,
Then is his grace sufficient for you,
that by his grace ye may be perfect in Christ."

—MORONI 10:32

When the war ended, most everyone went home, but he stayed on. My grandfather had been invited to play at Wimbledon, but he couldn't afford the ticket back to Europe from the United States, so he stayed. While he waited for the great tournament to begin, he spent time liberating the concentration camps in Germany. It's how he earned his keep. It's also where he contracted polio, just days before the tournament began.

He never played at Wimbledon.

Instead, he came home and locked himself in the back room for months and months.

She was patient with him. She took him his meals. She raised their girls. She was a haven in the midst of his anger, and she weathered his storms. When he finally came out of the dark and applied for a job, she got dressed and went to work with him. Her role was to push the wheelchair; she was the walking he couldn't do. He coached young boys into national champions, and she stood on the sideline of every court and cheered him on.

It's no wonder that she introduced him to God. Maybe at first, he believed because she did. If God was important to her, then God was important to him, because she was everything to him. In the end, his passion for God was equal to hers. Over time he proved the Lord, and the Lord was there. The same way she had always been.

Right with him all along.

I've never witnessed a love as thick as theirs. Inseparable. Lives intertwined.

There was that time they came to stay. I was a senior in high school. They journeyed three states to get to us, and travel was so hard on him. I gave up my room, because it was on the ground floor and there were no stairs, and it was easier for a wheelchair. But my room only had two twin beds, and it was fine, and they would make do.

Early the next morning, I had to sneak into that room. I had forgotten my toothbrush, and school was starting, and my mom said to just go in quietly. It was so early. Soft morning light spilled in through the windows, and that's how I made my way. I peeked over to see if I had woken anyone on my way back out and noticed my grandmother's bed was empty. I looked around the room to find her, but she wasn't sitting on the little blue sofa or the green chair in the corner. I looked to the other twin bed to see if Grandpa was still asleep, *and there she was*. Snuggled up tight and cuddled in, the two were one.

Theirs is the greatest love story of my life.
It is what I want in the end.
The giving up of what might come between.
An unselfish effort to live in love.

What does this have to do with Jesus?
Everything.

In the end, becoming isn't about work, or earning, or checklists or routine; this process of becoming is about love, and covenant, and relationship. We must remember love.

The giving up of what might come between.

⊕ ⊕ ⊕

It was in a time of tribulation that Paul wrote to the Saints in Ephesus. "For this cause I bow my knees unto the Father," he wrote, "that he would grant you . . . to be strengthened with might by his Spirit in the inner man" (Ephesians 3:14, 16). What a beautiful prayer for a time of trial. This idea of being strengthened with might hints of enabling grace, and I am immediately intrigued at the role the Spirit might play in helping us to receive the Savior's grace. I pause in my reading to consider the relationship of grace and the Spirit and am reminded of the line from a general conference talk that rang so true, hit home so precisely, spoke so loudly I can't remember anything else from that message except this one truth: *The Holy Ghost is the messenger of grace.*[19] If the Holy Ghost is truly the messenger of grace, I find myself wanting to improve my relationship with Him.

To give up what might come between.

"Hear the Word, search the Scriptures, read good books, receive the sacraments, pray; confer, for these be as so many conduits whereby the Creator conveyeth grace into the soul of the creature."[20] I am so interested in these conduits whereby the Creator conveyeth grace. I read through them and see how they are actions that lead to an increase of the Spirit, how they are rhythms of grace. When I read my scriptures, when I hear God's word, when I take the sacrament and pray, I experience an increase of the Spirit. I know how that feels. Paul is helping me to understand that with an increase of the Spirit I also experience an increase of grace. He describes the synergy of the two working together, how we can be *strengthened with might by the Spirit.* Could exalting grace combined with the influence of the Holy Ghost be influential in transforming someone into the divine life? "On the covenant path we also find the essential blessings. . . . This is help that can come only through divine grace, administered by the Holy Ghost."[21]

Elder Parley P. Pratt described the ability of the Holy Ghost to strengthen and transform: "The gift of the Holy Ghost . . . quickens all the intellectual faculties, increases, enlarges, expands, and purifies all the natural passions and affections, and adapts them, by the gift of wisdom, to their lawful use. It inspires, develops, cultivates, and matures all the fine-toned sympathies, joys, tastes, kindred feelings, and affections of our nature. It inspires virtue, kindness, goodness, tenderness, gentleness, and charity. It develops beauty of person, form, and features. It tends to health, vigor, animation, and social feeling. It invigorates all the faculties of the physical and intellectual man. It strengthens and gives tone to the nerves. In short, it is, as it were, marrow to the bone, joy to the heart, light to the eyes, music to the ears, and life to the whole being."[22]

The knowledge makes me want to spend more time in those activities that become a conduit of both the Spirit and grace. I begin to realize that walking the covenant path increases the privileges that flow from the blessings of the gospel because the ordinances and covenants lead to an increase of the Spirit. The increase of the Spirit leads to an increase of grace. By walking a covenant path, we can receive *greater* guidance, *greater* protection, and *greater* inspiration. That is the privilege of allowing His Spirit into the inner man, of becoming heirs of the Abrahamic covenant. "God provides an almost incomprehensible gift to help covenant-makers be covenant-keepers: the gift of the Holy Ghost."[23]

The promise is for His Spirit to be with us always.

Receiving the fulness of the blessing will require me to spend more time with Him. To improve my relationship. To increase my love. I turn back to Ephesians and realize Paul is not done with his discourse. In fact, we are about to arrive at my favorite verses. Now Paul teaches that as we are strengthened with might by his Spirit in the inner man, "Christ may dwell in your hearts by faith; that ye, being rooted and grounded in love, May be able to comprehend with all saints what is the breadth, and length, and depth, and height; And to know the love of Christ, which passeth knowledge, *that ye might be filled with all the fulness of God*" (Ephesians 3:17–20; emphasis added).

To be rooted and grounded in love for Him, to *know* the love of Christ fills us with all the fulness of God. All the fulness of God can also be defined as all that the Father has, which can also be defined as exaltation.

It is the relationship that leads to exaltation.

The walking of the covenant path with Him, the rhythm of the conduits of grace from His Spirit, the becoming rooted and grounded in His love—this is how we receive the grace that exalts us. This is what will enable us to become transformed. *It is all about the relationship.*

I am reminded again of the man who came home from the war and locked himself in the back bedroom and of the woman who loved him.

Suddenly I know how she knew what to do.

She lived her covenants, she practiced the especially active compassion she had learned from the Savior, she filled her life with conduits of grace to give her enabling strength to weather the storms, and she practiced charity because she was rooted and grounded in the pure love of Christ.

Walking the covenant path of exalting grace had transformed her into the companion my grandfather needed her to be. She was strengthened by might through His Spirit, and it enabled her to lift and strengthen another. More than she would have ever asked for or thought. His power working within her.

"Now unto him that is able to do exceeding abundantly above all that we ask or think, according to *the power that worketh in us,* Unto him be glory" (Ephesians 3:20–21; emphasis added).

Maybe you could stop for a minute and consider your own path, your own story, this particular moment in your life. Is what you want in the end worth the giving up of what might come between? Is it worth yielding your heart to Him? Because exaltation is to *know* the love of Christ. The breadth, and length, and depth, and height.

Exaltation is to know Christ.
To invest in loving Him.
To give up anything that might come between.

It is the relationship.

chapter eleven

THE GUIDE

*"Because of the Savior's Atonement,
His gospel provides an invitation to keep changing,
growing, and becoming more pure. It is a gospel of hope,
of healing, and of progress."*

—RUSSELL M. NELSON[24]

"In the beginning God created . . ." (Genesis 1:1).

From the void, from the place without form, out of the inky darkness, God moved, and through a process of progression the earth was made. Day one brought light out of darkness, next came the separation of earth from heaven, on the third day water and dry land appeared along with grasses, herbs, and fruit trees. Day four brought forth lights for signs, seasons, days, and years—we see the sun, moon, and stars, and we remember. On day five the waters brought forth abundantly—great whales and fish and living creatures that moved—but this was not all; He also imagined into reality bright-colored birds to fly above the earth. Day six brought forth the living creatures on the land, including everything that creepeth (see Genesis 1:1–25). The Creation was a process of progression. Each day's new gift introduced because of the preparation of the day before—one building upon the other, line upon line, precept upon precept. In Genesis we discover a godly pattern for growth and becoming and progression.

Within the beautiful imagery of the Creation, in the midst of every step, there is an oft-repeated phrase. We see it for the first time after day one: "And God saw the light, that it was good" (Genesis 1:4). It's there again on day three, after the waters and land were separated: "God saw that it was good" (v. 10). Four more times within the process, scripture records a similar phrase. "And God saw that it was good" (vv. 12, 18, 21, 25).

It is my nature to wait until the project is completed, until the work is finished, to evaluate whether or not my work is good. It is always in the end that I step back to evaluate the finished work and determine its worth.

Not God.

He saw the goodness in every step of the progression. He spoke it out loud. On day one, and twice on day three, and again there on day four. From the story of the Creation, we learn that our Father is just as interested in day-to-day progress as He is in the finished product. I think sometimes we forget that is true. We wonder if we are enough, if we are failing, if we are falling behind. We become discouraged. We doubt. We consider giving up. We must remember that God never expected the results of day six on day two. On day two, He was thrilled with the results of day two. He declared it good.

Why do we put the pressure on ourselves to become complete today instead of embracing the idea of progression? A little at a time. Every day better. Grace for grace. What if exaltation is all about progression?

Our God knows about line upon line. He sees where you have come from. He knows what you had to do to simply get through this day. If He were to whisper down from heaven tonight as you drift off to sleep, do you know what I think He would tell you?

You are already good.

⊕ ⊕ ⊕

For just a minute, let's consider what this process of progression looks like. Progression is the reason we left the security of heaven; we knew we could not progress any further without a body and the experiences of mortality. That progress was so important to us that we agreed to come without knowing what our journey would hold, how long it would last, or what the finished result would be. For most of us, this mortal journey will take longer than the six days of

Creation, but one similarity remains—God will say the same thing of you on day 692 as He did on day 3.

He will see the good.

The Father's greatest desire for us is to return home to Him, but returning home will require a process of progression. Just like in the story of the Creation, in life we discover a godly pattern for growth and becoming and progression. Each day delivers new gifts because of the preparation of the day before—one building upon the other, line upon line, precept upon precept. What does this progression eventually lead to? A fulness of happiness. His happiness. "When we feel insignificant, cast off, and forgotten, we learn that we may be assured that God has not forgotten us—in fact, that He offers to all His children something unimaginable: to become "heirs of God, and joint-heirs with Christ. . . . It is so humbling to know that this magnificent and supernal future is possible—not because of who we are but because of who God is. Knowing this, how . . . could we ever keep our eyes on the ground when the King of kings invites us to take flight into an unimaginable future of divine happiness? If we repent, mistakes do not disqualify us. They are part of our progress. We are all infants compared to the beings of glory and grandeur we are designed to become."[25]

At the end of this journey, heaven awaits. Scripture describes that final destination by introducing kingdoms; we call the highest kingdom exaltation. Sometimes the thought of those kingdoms overwhelms us. We wonder if we will ever measure up. We fear falling short. We forget the goodness God sees in us every single day. I think our Father knew we would forget, that we would consider ourselves incapable of returning perfect. He is the same God who knew about the darkness that wanted to overcome the light and the stormy seas that threatened to overwhelm the land, but the Father also knew about the multiplying and the replenishing and the finding joy.

In the beginning, God created . . .

He knew we would measure ourselves against ourselves and compare ourselves among ourselves, and He knew that wouldn't be wise. He did not want us to stretch ourselves beyond our capacity, so He created "a measure to reach even unto you" (2 Corinthians 10:13).

I find so much comfort in that verse.

But that is not all. He sent His Son to help us navigate the path. One who could make up the difference and strengthen our weak parts. The author and the finisher who would enable us to fulfill the measure of our creation (see Hebrews 12:1–3). He did not send us here to journey alone. To fail. To fall short. His work and His glory are to bring us home to His highest kingdom (see Moses 1:39), to the place where we can experience all that the Father has, a place filled with happiness.

Every one of us has the opportunity to reach the highest kingdom, exaltation, through a divine plan of progression, increase, growth, and becoming. To ensure our success, the Father sent His Son to accompany us every step of the way and designed a covenant path to allow increased revelation and relationship with Him. He knew every step of our journey would be a process of creation. The elevating of a soul always is.

I look back again at the Creation story and notice one truth I want to keep in the forefront of my own story: Not only does our Father plan to be part of my personal creating and finishing process; He plans to bless me and remind me of my good along the way (see Genesis 1:28, 31).

Every single day.

⊕ ⊕ ⊕

Every time I walk down Disneyland's Main Street, I tear up. I can't help it. It's because of Walt, mostly. Because how many people do you know who devote their entire life's work to bring to pass someone else's happiness?

This time when we walk under the tunnel that leads to Main Street, I am already preparing for the tears to flow. Not happy tears. It's been a hard season, one of our hardest in recent years. I came here to remind myself that there still was a happy place somewhere in the world. I take my time walking. I read the signs on the windows. For some reason, the job descriptions written on those signs lift my heart. On the second story of one of the shops, there is a blue-trimmed window with a white lace curtain. Black words are stenciled there on the window: "Roger Broggie. Shopmaster. Advisor to the Magic Makers." I am reminded of a favorite quote. "Make no small plans, they have no magic to stir men's souls."[26] And I think how much I need a magic-maker in my life. This soul needs stirring.

At the end of Main Street there is a red brick firehouse. No. 105. A brass bell hangs from the top of the building. I have never heard it ring. Just under the bell there is a window framed with decorative block, the shade pulled down halfway. The white curtains on either side hang open, framing the little lamp sitting there on the table. The lamp is always on. That little lamp has shone through the window since the day after Walt died. It is a reminder of the man who stood there at the window every day to watch the families making happy memories below. A witness that his spirit, his hope, his magic lives on. I need some of that magic right now.

We have been given this trip as a gift from a good friend. He set aside the tickets for us at will call. He knows how hard this season has been. When he calls to tell me about the tickets, he explains he has also asked for a guide to accompany us for the day. I tell him we don't really need a guide. He tells me to just accept the guide. "You will be grateful at the end," he tells me. He is a good friend, so I trust him.

Our envelope with the tickets is deep navy blue with scrolling on the outside. The gold tab on the back has our name and a date, January 9, 2019. I still have the envelope. I never want to forget what I learned about kingdoms on that day. Our guide in the checkered vest meets us first thing that morning. He asks our names, and then we start off. The man knows everything about Disneyland. As we walk, he shares stories and insights and mysteries. When we get to each attraction, he takes us to a private entrance, and we walk right on to the ride. He rides with us—in case we have questions, in case we want to go again, to make sure we lack for nothing. He takes us to his favorite restaurant for lunch, tells us the best places for treats, and shows us the tiny house by the trunk of the large tree next to the Indiana Jones ride that I would have never noticed on my own. At the end of the day, he takes us to stand under the window of the red brick firehouse at No. 105. He is the one who told me about the lamp.

On that day we experienced the fulness of the privileges the Magic Kingdom has to offer.

It is one of my best days. I won't ever forget it. The guide, the rest from the weary, the magic.

It was just what my soul needed.

When we left, I told Greg that was the best Disneyland trip possible and we could never ever forget the goodness of it, because we would never experience it again. I tucked my special envelope inside my suitcase for safekeeping, with the unfathomable hope that maybe one day we would take our whole family there and let them experience that kind of magic. A fulness of happiness.

It was several months later that I was studying the kingdoms in section 76. The entirety of salvation. The description of heaven. I had listed each kingdom out, the way we do. Different privileges according to our different choices. If you were to make the list, perhaps it would look something like this:

A TELESTIAL LIFE: No gospel, no testimony of Jesus, no prophet, no covenants. The privilege of the light of Christ. These are people who will choose to pay for their own sin and to believe in Christ's saving grace only to the extent that they will overcome hell and be taken to the telestial kingdom by virtue of the cross (see D&C 76:81–89; 19:15–19; 2 Nephi 9:8–10; Matthew 5:26; 1 Corinthians 15:22; Alma 34:15–16).

A TERRESTRIAL LIFE: A belief in Christ, in His gospel, and in scripture, but a life without restored law, without priesthood ordinances, without covenants. These people experience the privilege of the *power* of the Holy Ghost and receive saving grace through belief in Christ to overcome sin (see D&C 76:71–80; Alma 34:13–41; Romans 5:1–2, 9; 10:9–10; Moses 6:60; "Holy Ghost," Guide to the Scriptures).

A CELESTIAL LIFE: A belief in the restored gospel of Jesus Christ, the fulness of His scripture, baptism by one who holds authority, priesthood ordinances, and temple covenants. These people experience the privilege of the *gift* of the Holy Ghost and receive Christ's exalting grace in order to become like Him (see D&C 76:51–69; 20:30–31; 1 Corinthians 15:40–43; 6:11; 2 Nephi 31; Moroni 10:33; 3 Nephi 27:20; Alma 5:54; 13:12; Ether 12:27).

Finally, we learn of EXALTATION, the living of an exalted life. These people experience the privilege of the fulness of the gospel, the fulness of priesthood, all that the Father has. They have been sealed to a spouse, received the fulness of the new and everlasting covenant, the Holy Spirit of Promise, and the Second Comforter. These receive His exalting grace in order to become glorified (see D&C 132:19–21, 37; Ephesians 4:13, 24; John 14:18, 21, 23; Moroni 10:32). This is the fulness of the covenant path. This is the kingdom promised to Abraham.

Some people read section 76 and see these kingdoms as a final destination, a place where we will arrive after the Day of Judgment. But what if these kingdom verses also describe a way of living here and now? A process of progression. Could mortality be a practice ground for becoming in preparation for the eventual kingdom we will receive?

It was the Pharisees who asked the Lord when the kingdom of God should come. He told them not to look for it, how they wouldn't see it, "for, behold, the kingdom of God is within you" (Luke 17:20–21). The Lord taught that the kingdom of God isn't something to watch or wait for; it is something we become. Could the same be true of exaltation?

When I read section 76, I see a pattern, a process of progress and increase that can take place over time here in mortality to help prepare us for heaven. Upward and forward. I begin to recognize how the action of belief combined with an increase of the Spirit and the enabling power of exalting grace can transform us, grace for grace. I see how we have the potential to ascend upward and forward here in mortality through the Spirit and His grace as we respond to His call to become (see D&C 93:20). It is the privilege of living the law of God here on the earth and the process of being made righteous through belief, the Spirit, and grace in preparation for what is to come.

Like Abraham, my spirit longs for the fulness of the highest kingdom. I desperately yearn to take my family there, to experience the fulness of happiness that will only be found in exaltation. I recognize that what sets the privileges of each kingdom apart is my own willingness to believe in the gospel and act in faith, to allow the influence of the Spirit to work within me, and to receive both saving and exalting grace along the way. I begin to understand that exaltation is something we practice for. We don't reach a fulness overnight. Progression cannot be achieved on our own merit; it requires His work in us.

I must remember that.

Because sometimes the kingdom list overwhelms me. I wonder if I will be good enough, righteous enough, worthy enough. *I wonder if I will ever be enough.* More than anything, I want to experience His happiness. But I have to remind myself that there is a process to progression. Every time I wake up in the morning, I whisper a favorite phrase, *every day better.* It's what I tell myself over and over again. If I can just be a little bit better than I was yesterday then I know I am progressing, I am on the path to exaltation, to the Father's fulness. To His happiness. If I look to Him throughout this process, He will remind me of my goodness along the way.

That's the kingdom experience I want to have. But how will I find my way there? My mind reflects back to my Magic Kingdom experience, and suddenly I see a similarity. I almost refused the guide, thinking I could navigate it on my own.

What if I had refused the guide?

The same is true here. I have been offered a Guide who knows my name and who knows everything about this adventure I am on. He has stories to share with me, and insights, and mysteries. He is willing to accompany me on every ride—the thrillers, the heart stoppers, the ones that make me laugh out loud, and the quiet excursions filled with song that fill me with peace and allow reflection. He is there in case I have questions, in case I need blessings, to make sure I lack nothing (see Deuteronomy 2:7). He is strength, and tender mercy, and constant guidance. When times are dark,

He will remind me of the light and a Father who stands at the window to watch all of the families below. A Father who offers a clear path and His Spirit and His grace and mercies and miracles.

A Father who wants nothing more than for us to experience His fulness.

It's why He offered His Son.
To guide us, to give us the gift of His grace.

And what if I passed up on His grace?

After I finish my studies, I dig through my drawer of memories to find the deep navy envelope with the beautiful scrolls and the golden tab. I place it carefully in section 76 so I will remember that I want more than just the promise of salvation. I want Abraham's promise; I want to experience the fulness of the Father. I want the blessings of the highest kingdom. I determine to walk the covenant path of exaltation with Christ. To embrace everything He offers me. In the end, I know I will be grateful for the Guide because He knows better than I ever will how to return me back to the One who creates magic. The One who knows how to stir men's souls. The One who sees me and knows that I am good, who waits anxiously for my return.

In the end, I want to return to the One who has devoted His entire eternal work to bring to pass the eternal happiness of His family.

chapter twelve

TO BECOME

"I came unto mine own, and mine own received me not;
But unto as many as received me gave I power to do many miracles,
And to become the sons of God;
And even unto them that believed on my name
gave I power to obtain eternal life."

—DOCTRINE AND COVENANTS 45:8

We saw him bundled up in his black coat, walking through the neighborhood one morning in March. My friend is the epitome of wisdom with a wealth of doctrinal insight. He has served within the highest councils. I believe he is one of God's finest teachers. We stopped to talk, and he began to walk with us along our familiar path. The subject of revelation came up, and we couldn't help but ask for his wisdom there. *The older I get*, he started, his soft voice filled with humility as he turned to both of us to make sure we were listening, *the less I know. It seems the Lord is always growing us. There is always more to learn. Sometimes it is a struggle.*

It wasn't what I had expected.

For some reason his words brought my soul great relief. I am half a century old. I am so grateful to know that I don't need to be an expert yet, that the Lord is always growing us, will continue to grow us. That there is always more to learn.

Perhaps the relief came because there are things in me that need fixing. No matter how hard I try, it seems I still struggle and fight to get things right. There are places I feel raw and undone. I want to think every year brings me nearer to being complete, but in reality, most times I feel like I'm falling short. What I recognize most in myself is my brokenness. How much I don't know. How much I still need to learn.

In the summertime I drive a 1975 yellow Jeep. No doors. Canvas top. The steering wheel is on the wrong side of the car. I love that Jeep. When my grandson Luka comes to visit, he starts yelling the word "Jeep" right when he walks in the front door. He is two years old and he doesn't have a great mastery of very many words, but he knows that word. He loves the yellow Jeep just as much as I do.

In August, the Jeep broke down. It was just the battery, but it took several days to fix. Luka was devastated. Every time he walked in the house, I had to explain to him that we couldn't go for a ride because the Jeep was broken. He quickly learned a new word. *Broken*. It wasn't long before he learned two more new words: *fix it*.

He would wander around my house saying that little phrase over and over again. "Jeep. Broken. Fix it." It made me smile.

One day, in the midst of the Jeep-fixing shenanigans, I heard Luka come running through the family room. At barely two years old he is also still trying to master running. He crashed headfirst into the wooden table next to the couch and immediately started crying. I came running from my bedroom and his dad came running from the basement just in time to hear him say, "I broken, Nana. Fix it."

I wonder if you've ever felt broken?

Maybe it's your will that feels broken. Maybe your heart. Perhaps it is your faith. Maybe you don't even know what it is that is broken; you just know something isn't right. He comes with courage, kindness, and comfort. He comes with understanding. He knows how to care for you, even in the moments when you aren't your best. Jesus comes into the places that are raw. Wounded. Strained. He comes into the places where we struggle.

He knows how to fix it.

"The Spirit of the Lord is upon me, because he hath anointed me to preach the gospel to the poor; *he hath sent me to heal the brokenhearted,* to preach deliverance to the captives, and recovering of sight to the blind" (Luke 4:18; emphasis added).

"To comfort all that mourn . . . to give unto them beauty for ashes, the oil of joy for mourning, the garment of praise for the spirit of heaviness" (Isaiah 61:2–3).

Show me a broken soul, you might say, and I will show you a woman sitting at her well, a leper separated from his family, and a daughter lying at the point of death in her bedroom. I will show you a boy who tries to jump into raging fires and drown himself in any water he finds. I will show you a man who wanders through the tombs, cutting himself, and I will show you how Jesus shows up in every one of those stories.

The Jesus I know is not afraid of broken.

It is our brokenness that draws Him to us, and us to Him. It is why we turn to Him for lifting. It is through our brokenness that His exalting grace is best made manifest. It is through the struggle that we discover Him.

I won't soon forget the unique opportunity that has been ours to participate in the ordinance of the sacrament each week in the family room of our home. I once returned home just after everything had been prepared but before the prayer had been spoken. I wanted to be part of what was about to take place, but I wasn't sure if they had included me in their preparation. "Is there enough for me?" I asked as I settled into the yellow chair that is my favorite place in our home.

"Everything can be broken, Mom."

It was my daughter's immediate response, and as I waited for the prayer to begin, I realized it was true. It is the breaking that allows for more to be given. As I closed my eyes, I thought of every broken piece of bread, one for each of us in that room, and how each piece could be broken into more, if needed. How we wouldn't run out.

I had never realized until that moment that broken could equal more.

Maybe, when we think of the Savior's grace, we ask the same question. Is there enough for me? Do we remember we are asking it of the One who was broken for us on Calvary? Was it His willingness to be broken that allows that grace to be so freely given? If broken equals more, then we never have to wonder again if there will be enough.

Because as long as we have Jesus, there is.

It is January 2020. I walk into her house and hear her struggle to breathe. I see how she fights for every breath, how she is laboring to stay on this side of the veil, and I know she won't be with us long. I watch her fingers turning white with death. We hold her hands and feel her coldness as she begins slipping to the other side. It is hard to die. Painfully hard. In those last hours, watching her struggle exhausts every one of us. We see how the cancer has ravaged her body, how it has taken her eyes, and her hearing, and now her ability to even breathe. I look at her worn-out body and see how this has broken her.

And then, it is over.

Sweet peace fills the room. There is a weighted silence there. The silence is more profound because of the struggle that preceded it. The struggle that has exhausted all of us. We rest in the silent peace, eyes drawn to her.

Death reminds you of how short mortality really is, this leaving the presence of God for a time. As I look at her, lying there, still, my mind reflects on the struggle of her mortality, the mountains she climbed, the story she wrote with her living. Our conversations about Jesus, how He meets us where we are. I remember the afternoon after the surgery to remove her eyes, when she asked me to remember that when I talk of His grace, I must teach that He descended lower than us all, lower than the pain we will ever suffer in mortality, so He can lift us (see D&C 88:6). I realize she knew from experience what she was testifying of, how He lifted her. The conversation of our life was filled with our struggles, our lack, our want, and God's promise. I look at her and realize that it was her breaking that allowed more to be given. I saw how His Spirit was mighty in the strengthening of her, how His grace had carried her through failures and fear. My best conversations about Jesus happened at her bedside.

Do you know those moments when your lips quiver with the holding back, when your tears spill over, when the hurt in your chest almost suffocates you?

It happens when you realize one of God's greatest encouragers has been taken home.

That night we stood in solemn silence. Reverent. Knowing what we had lost.

Then someone whispered, "Here lies one of the noble and great ones," and we saw how it was true. It is her brokenness that qualified her for that tribute.

It was the broken that made her noble.

It caused her to become great.

His covenant path had exalted her. Through the walking of it, she became as He is. We all watched it happen through the years. We all saw how she wasted and wore out her life in pursuit of Him. How He completed her.

Now her journey gives me courage to continue mine.

I see the storm clouds rolling in, I watch the wind sifting through the stalks of wheat, I walk through the field in my bright yellow dress with a rustic, red ladder in hand.

Just there, in the middle of the storm clouds raging, I begin to climb.

On the third rung from the top, I look up to the heavens.

I know He will meet me where I am, as I am.
He has met me here before.

The same way I trust He will lift me to where He is, as He is.

I am coming to understand His process for the elevating of a soul.

On this stormy afternoon, reaching out to fully embrace His grace along my own covenant path becomes paramount.

So, I stretch wide my arms.

And just there, through a break in the dark clouds, the glitter of His gift showers down.

Grace to become.

I reach up, and my soul takes flight.

When you climb up a ladder,
you must begin at the bottom and ascend
step by step
until you arrive at the top,
and so it is with the principles of the Gospel—
you must begin with the first,
and go on
until you learn all the principles of exaltation;
but it will be a great while
after you have passed through the vail
before you will have learned them.
It is not all to be comprehended in this world;
it will be a great work
to learn our salvation and exaltation
even beyond the grave.

—JOSEPH SMITH[27]

NOTES

1. "Discourse on Abbatôn by Timothy, Archbishop of Alexandria," in *Coptic Martyrdoms etc. in the Dialect of Upper Egypt*, ed. and trans. E. A. Wallis Budge (1914), 482. Timothy, archbishop of Alexandria, died in AD 385. Brackets are included in Budge's English translation.

2. Dieter F. Uchtdorf, "The Gift of Grace," *Ensign*, May 2015.

3. See Tad R. Callister, *The Infinite Atonement* (Salt Lake City: Deseret Book, 2000), 263–68, 276–77; see also https://www.ldsliving.com/Grace-One-Profound-Explanation-That-Will-Answer-Your-Questions/s/89726.

4. Russell M. Nelson, "Endure and Be Lifted Up," *Ensign*, May 1997.

5. All Hebrew meanings are taken from *Strong's Concordance*.

6. "Genesis 15: A Covenant Confirmed," *Old Testament Seminary Student Study Guide* (2002), 24–25.

7. Alfred Edersheim, *History of the Bible* Vol. 1, 90.

8. Dieter F. Uchtdorf, "The Gift of Grace," *Ensign*, May 2015.

9. R. S. Thomas, ed., "The Coming," in *Collected Poems* (London: Orion Books, 1972), 234.

10. Joseph F. Smith, *Gospel Doctrine*, 84.

11. Joy D. Jones, "An Especially Noble Calling," *Ensign*, May 2020.

12. C. S. Lewis, *Mere Christianity* (New York: Touchstone, 1996), 175–76.

13. Eugene H. Peterson, translator, Matthew 11:28–30 in *The Message: The Bible in Contemporary Language* (Colorado Springs: NavPress, 2005); emphasis added; see also https://www.biblegateway.com/passage/?search=Matthew%2011%3A28-30&version=MSG.

14. See OED, 2nd ed.: grace(n), 11b.

15. David A. Bednar, "An Evening with a General Authority," April 10, 2020.

16. Jeffrey R. Holland, "Be Ye Therefore Perfect—Eventually," *Ensign*, Nov. 2017.

17. Bruce C. Hafen, "Beauty for Ashes: The Atonement of Jesus Christ," *Ensign*, Apr. 1990.

18. Pierre Teilhard de Chardin, SJ, "Patient Trust," in *Hearts on Fire* (Chicago: Loyola Press, 2004), 102.

19. See D. Todd Christofferson, "The Power of Covenants," *Ensign*, May 2009.

20. J. Barlow, D. D., The Biblical Illustrator, Electronic Database. Copyright 2002, 2003, 2006, 2011 by Biblesoft, Inc.

21. D. Todd Christofferson, "The Covenant Path," *Liahona*, May 2021.

22. Parley P. Pratt, *Key to the Science of Theology and a Voice of Warning*, 61.

23. D. Todd Christofferson, "The Covenant Path," *Liahona*, May 2021.

24. Russell M. Nelson, "Welcome Message," *Liahona*, May 2021.

25. Dieter F. Uchtdorf, "God Is among Us," *Liahona*, May 2021.

26. Spencer W. Kimball, as quoted by Vaughn J. Featherstone, "The Last Drop in the Chalice," BYU devotional, September 24, 1985.

27. "History, 1838–1856, volume E-1 [1 July 1843–30 April 1844]," p. 1971, The Joseph Smith Papers, accessed March 1, 2021, https://www.josephsmithpapers.org/paper-summary/history-1838-1856-volume-e-1-1-july-1843-30-april-1844/343; see also *History of the Church* 6:306–7.

ABOUT THE AUTHOR

EMILY BELLE FREEMAN is a best-selling author and popular inspirational speaker. She has a deep love of the scriptures, which comes from a desire to find their application in everyday life. She is the author of numerous books, including *Grace Where You Are*; *Creating a Christ-Centered Home*; *Closer to Christ*; and *Even This: Getting to the Place Where You Can Trust God with Anything.* She is a favorite speaker at Time Out for Women and a cohost with David Butler of *Don't Miss This,* a "Come, Follow Me" study channel on YouTube. Her greatest joy comes from spending time with her family. Read more at emilybellefreeman.com and follow Emily on Instagram and Facebook @emilybellefreeman.